From Slaves to Soldiers

The SIEGE OF RHODE ISLAND, taken from Mr. Brindley's House,
on the 25th of August 1778.

The 1st Rhode Island
Regiment in the
American Revolution

From
Slaves
TO
Soldiers

Robert A. Geake

*with Lorén M. Spears, Executive Director,
Tomaquag Museum*

WESTHOLME
Yardley

Westholme Publishing, LLC
904 Edgewood Road
Yardley, Pennsylvania 19067
Visit our Web site at www.westholmepublishing.com

ISBN: 978-1-59416-415-6
Also available as an eBook.

Printed in the United States of America

Contents

List of Illustrations

Authors' Note

OF THE HEROES REMEMBERED FROM RHODE ISLAND who served in the Revolutionary War, perhaps none hold such a compelling, collective story as those men of the 1st Rhode Island Regiment, which would become popularly known as the "black regiment." The Honorable Tristam Burges, representative of Rhode Island, would tell Congress in 1828 that, "No braver men met the enemy in battle, but not one was permitted to be a soldier until he had first been made a freeman."

In his speech Burges referenced those slaves who enlisted to earn their freedom, but the 1st Rhode Island Regiment was much more than those former slaves. Indeed, the regiment was an amalgamation of poor white laborers and farm boys, free blacks, and indigenous men, as well as slaves and indentured servants. It was a regiment whose role in the revolution was nearly forgotten, whose veterans witnessed the growth of a new republic, but whose own fortunes would be bound in the continuing struggle for freedom and equality.

We hope in the following pages to elaborate upon the known story of the 1st Rhode Island Regiment, to go beyond the battles and officers, to reach the common men who enlisted, as well as the slaves, and tell as best we can their story before and after the Revolutionary War.

Rhode Island and the Providence Plantations, 1776. Moving from north to south, the major towns at this time were Providence, Warwick, Bristol, Greenwich, and on the south end of Rhode Island itself, Newport. (*Library of Congress*)

I

The Origins of the
1st Rhode Island Regiment

RHODE ISLAND AT THE ONSET OF THE AMERICAN Revolution was a jewel among the rough-hewn colonies of British America. In Kings County, princely estates lay along the southern shores of Narragansett Bay. From the water, newcomers would have seen great swaths of cleared meadows dotted with sheep and cattle, hayfields, cornfields, gardens, and orchards all bordered by stone walls, wooden fences, and boxwood hedges. These farms comprised thousands of acres and exported horses, oxen, sheep, pigs, bricks, lumber, and other goods at a prodigious rate, due to the labor of both indigenous men and imported African slaves.

Inland from these impressive estates, great stands of timber stretched back as far as the eye could see, broken only by the small communities grown along the rivers for industry, and the farm villages carved out of the wilderness off a well-traveled road. The smallest colony also held an international port city in Newport, on the island of Aquidneck, often named "Rhode Island" on maps of the period, and the landing site of hundreds of slave ships by the time of the war with Great Britain. The commercial port along the Providence River, Providence, swelled with merchant ships, cargo barges, and slave ships as well, and between the two settlements, scores of private docks stretched out from the shore onto Narragansett Bay, the gateway to commerce and fortune.

In Parliament, it was generally viewed that much of the wealth of the colony had been gained by the merchant ships shirking payment of the duties on goods with the bypassing of main ports and their customs officers, and thus smuggling in those goods to secret locations on shore. Merchant captains were also suspected of offloading wares on one of the many islands that dotted the shoreline inland from the larger islands of Jamestown and Newport in the south, to the seaside communities of East Greenwich, Warwick, and Pawtuxet on the western side of Narragansett Bay, and Bristol, Warren, and Barrington on the eastern shore, with Providence lying in the northernmost reaches of the Bay.

Indeed, a fair deal of smuggling goods and tax evasion occurred amid the bustling legal commerce of the colony. When Great Britain attempted to curtail these activities by harassing any and all ships they could in Narragansett Bay, Rhode Islanders responded in historic and unprecedented fashion. They boarded and burned one of the British navy ships harassing their merchant vessels to the waterline.

By the spring of 1772, the many ships, boats, ferries, and barges that plied the waters of Narragansett Bay were under intense scrutiny by a small fleet of British patrol ships. One of these was the HMS *Gaspee*, under command of Lieutenant William Dudingston, charged with patrolling the waters from Newport harbor to the north and Greenwich Bay, and on to Warwick and Conimicut, where the river narrowed and continued past Namquid Point in Pawtuxet, before leading to the capital city.

In March, the *Providence Gazette* had informed its readers that "A number of men belonging to the armed schooner that has been for some time past cruising in the river interrupting the traders, firing on Oyster boats and we are told landed on the Narragansett shore a few days since and carried off several Hogs belonging to the inhabitants, and also a Quantity of firewood."

On the afternoon of June 9, 1772, the *Gaspee* trailed the sloop *Hannah* as it sailed from Newport up the Bay toward Providence. The sloop was a vessel owned by William Greene of Potowomut, now part of Warwick, who had business dealings with the merchant John Brown of Providence.

The *Hannah* sailed past Namquid Point, from which extends a long sandbar just feet below the waves, nearly halfway across the passage of the river. The *Gaspee* ran hard aground, leaving it beached on the sandbar until the floodtide returned the next day.

That night, having heard of the ship's vulnerable position, a crowd of revelers gathered at the Sabin Tavern in Providence, and before midnight, some sixty men set off from Fenner's wharf in a fleet of eight longboats with muffled oars, and rowed the six nautical miles to the

Overleaf: "A Topographical Chart of the Bay of Narragansett in the Province of New England" by Charles Blaskowitz, 1777. "Gaspee Point" can be seen to the left of the word "River" in Providence River.

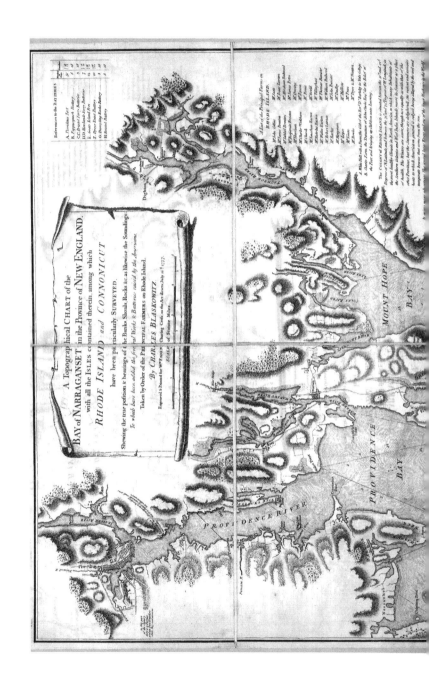

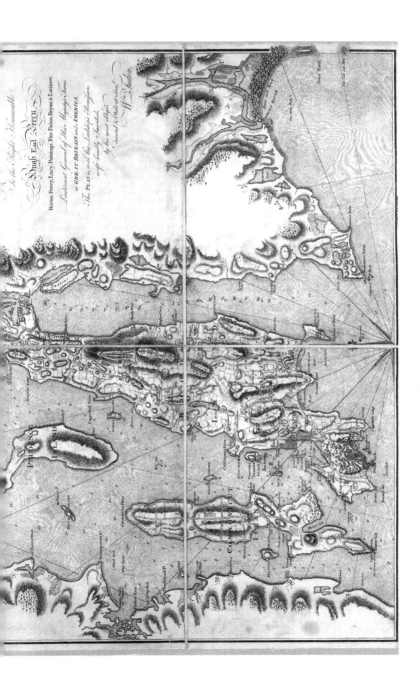

sandbar where the British ship lay aground. They were joined by men from Pawtuxet, some of whom would become part of the famed Pawtuxet Rangers during the war to come.

They fired upon the vessel, took the crew prisoner, pillaged the *Gaspee* of its goods, and set it ablaze. The Pawtuxet men rowed the captives to a dock by the still-house, before the main harbor of the town, where they were taken as prisoners to various houses, while the men from the Sabin Tavern rowed back to Providence by the light of the fire.

In the wake of the incident, amid British outrage and Rhode Island's seeming reluctance to offer much support in punishing those responsible, the communities in Providence, Washington, and Kent counties that comprised the colony began to reassemble or enlist militias for the common defense.

Some communities in the colony had established militias, many now filled with older veterans of the French and Indian War, but these had become mostly ceremonial units leading up to the revolution. By 1772, however, Rhode Island, like the other colonies, was teeming with young men anxious for a fight.

THE BEGINNINGS OF THE REGIMENT THAT BECAME THE 1ST Rhode Island may be said to have begun as one of these local militia, when a group of friends, including Nathanael Greene and James Mitchell Varnum, a lawyer who represented Greene's father's interests (including the *Hannah*), began meeting regularly at the home of William Arnold of East Greenwich. Arnold was involved in mercantile trade with French New Guinea and Surinam, as well as the coastal trade in the colonies.

Left, Nathanael Greene (1742–1786). (*National Park Service*) Right, James Mitchell Varnum (1748–1789) by John Nelson Arnold (1870). (*Brown University Portrait Collection*)

The two men formed, with a group of volunteers from Coventry, Warwick, and East Greenwich, a military company in preparation for war. They mustered on a regular basis but kept outside knowledge of the militia as clandestine as possible. Nathanael Greene often made the trip to Boston to see Henry Knox, a bookseller and later chief artillery officer in the Continental Army. In September 1774, Greene secretly purchased a new musket for himself on a visit to Boston, and while there, made the acquaintance of William Johnson, a British deserter, who agreed to return with Greene to Rhode Island and train his militia. Tensions were simmering in Kent County, as that same month in East Greenwich a riot had occurred in town, with some of the inhabitants burning an effigy of Judge Stephen Arnold of Warwick, for his alleged Tory sensibilities.

With this deserter's aid, the group began to drill and learn military tactics beyond what the young Greene could offer from his collection of military texts. In October 1774, James M. Varnum petitioned the state and was granted a charter to form the militia under the name of the Kentish Guard.

Soon the militia was meeting at Arnold's tavern, at the sign of the "Bunch of Grapes"[1] in East Greenwich, and mustering in the open—always a draw for young recruits. Nathanael Greene's East Greenwich cousin Christopher Greene had also joined and was named a lieutenant in the Guard, and later appointed major by the General Assembly in May 1775 for what was named "An army of Observation."[2]

The Kentish Guard would contribute two generals and at least three colonels to the Continental Army formed to fight the American Revolution. Varnum nearly quit the Guard when the regiment balked at naming Greene its commander. Greene had been born with a slight disability—one leg being shorter than the other—and he led the Guard in marches with a noticeable limp, a defect that to members was apparently unacceptable in a leader. His friend was understandably furious, but Greene persuaded him to honor his service. Varnum duly took command, and Nathanael Greene, the man who would become second in command to Washington, began his brief service as a private in the Kentish Guard.

When the "army of Observation" was called by the General Assembly to be recruited at various points throughout the colony, Varnum was assigned Kent and Kings counties as his area of recruitment, with Colonel Thomas Church recruiting in Bristol and Newport counties, as well as Colonel Daniel Hitchcock in Providence. Recruits could sign up for a bounty of $4.00 for six months' service. The regiment was officially organized on May 8, 1775, consisting of eight companies of volunteers.

Little more than a month later, Varnum marched the regiment to Roxbury, Massachusetts, where on June 14 it was formally adopted into the Continental Army. The regiment took part in the battle of Bunker Hill on June 16 and 17, and by late June it was reorganized into ten companies. Those of the Kentish Guard returned to Rhode Island where they spent twenty days in June guarding Warwick Neck, quartered at the old stone house of the Greene family. They spent another fifteen days at Quidnessett. In July the regiment was assigned to the brigade of General Nathanael Greene, in Washington's main army.

On January 1, 1776, the regiment was reorganized once again into eight companies and renamed the 9th Continental Regiment. The troops mustered then took part in the siege of Boston until March. Again, some returned to Warwick Neck, others were sent to Prudence Island. In May, members of the regiment and the Kentish Guard set out from East Greenwich Bay and retook a vessel that had been driven ashore and taken by two tenders of Captain James Wallace's fleet of the British navy. Wallace had threatened Newport for months and then bombarded the city when residents failed to comply with his demand for supplies. He was known to threaten other seaside communities along the bay as well.

On August 12, Nathanael Greene's brigade was re-designated as Nixon's Brigade, under command of Colonel John Nixon and comprising of the 9th and 11th Rhode Island, and the 4th and 12th Massachusetts regiments of the Continental Line. Nixon had served in the Massachusetts militia during the French and Indian War, and led the Sudbury militia in the battles of Lexington and Concord. His brigade would now take part in the long, grueling campaign in New York that summer and into the fall, and then continue the campaign into New Jersey at the onset of winter.

In January 1777, the Continental Army was regrouped, and the regiment reclaimed its name as the 1st Rhode Island Regiment. Varnum had been named brigadier general, and the regiment was now under the command of Nathanael Greene's cousin Colonel Christopher Greene.

Christopher Greene had been one of one hundred and fifty volunteers from Rhode Island to take part in the "Canadian Expedition" under command of Colonel Benedict Arnold, grandson of a famed tavern keeper and one-time governor of the colony. The young Arnold was ambitious as he mustered his men and gathered supplies. He was also ignorant, however, of the terrain through which he and his men would be traveling, and greatly underestimated the length of the march his men would face by some one hundred seventy miles.[3] Arnold's ill-fated "expedition" marched through rain and ice some forty-five days before they reached Quebec, with the troops suffering great hardships for the cold and lack of nourishment. Lieutenant Colonel John Percival recorded that, "We had nothing to support nature for seventeen days but one pint of flour per day for ten men, a dog's liver, entrails of a squirrel, and we were almost famished when relief came to us."[4]

Relief came by way of Commander Richard Montgomery of New York, who, after capturing Montreal, had marched some three hundred men with provisions and ammunition to where Arnold's troops lay anxiously waiting.

Quebec lay on a high, jagged peninsula that jutted out at the intersection of the St. Lawrence River and its tributary, the St. Charles River. Lower Town stretched along the narrow curve of land at the end of the peninsula, while on the southeastern slope lay Cape Diamond, some three hundred feet above the tide. Upper Town, as it was called, stood at the highest point of the steep cliffs, which protected the main part of the city on three sides. To the west stood a thirty-foot wall that extended from one river to the other.

Arnold's troops were malnourished, sick, and, by this time, suffering from low morale as well. It was the general's decision then, as historian Robert Middlekauff writes: "An assault rather than a siege had to be made. Arnold's soldiers from New England would not remain in the army after the end of the year when their enlistments expired. Even if they had been willing, they could not have sustained a siege for long because in the spring, when the ice melted in the St. Lawrence, transports carrying British soldiers would undoubtedly come up the river to relieve the city."[5]

Twenty-four-year-old William Humphrey, a veteran of the Rhode Island Regiment, was part of the expedition and recorded the events leading up to the assault:

> December 30 This day the enemy kept up a smart fire all day upon St. Roques but did little or no damage; this evening about 10 o'clock received orders that it was the general determination to storm the city of Quebec; then we ordered our men to get their arms in readiness for to go and storm; it was very dark and snowed We were to receive a signal by 3 skyrockets when to attack, but not observing them, we was about 1/2 hour too late; Capt. Dearborn's company, on account of being quartered on the other side of the [St.] Charles River and tide being high, not coming up, however, we proceeded without them.

Arnold gathered some six hundred troops early on the morning of December 31, and moved on the northern side of Lower Town, with Montgomery taking three hundred men for an assault on the south. A blizzard whipped snow in the men's faces as they marched, and temperatures plummeted. Arnold's men reached the walls at five o'clock and managed to take the guard at that point easily, but as the troops stormed into the town, Humphrey would write, "they fired very briskly upon us; we passed along the street and they killed and wounded a number of our men; . . . after we gained the first barrier, we rallied our men and tried to take the second barrier, and notwithstanding their utmost efforts, we got some of our ladders up [but] was obliged to retreat, which we did to first barrier we had took, and when we came there we found we could not retreat without losing all our men or at least the most of them."[6]

Arnold was wounded in the leg and carried from the field. His second in command Daniel Morgan rallied the troops for the second wave, but as Humphrey indicates in his journal, the battle was already lost.

Montgomery's forces had splintered as well, the commander being among the first to fall. Within but a few hours, four hundred Americans had been taken prisoner, Christopher Greene among them, and another fifty or sixty men dead or wounded.[7]

GREENE SPENT EIGHT MONTHS AS A PRISONER BEFORE AN exchange set him and others free. A short time after his release, he was appointed commander of the Rhode Island Regiment and sent with the 2nd Rhode Island Regiment to take part in the defense of the Delaware River. In May, they were in Morristown, New Jersey, and then marched to Fort Montgomery in August. By October, Colonel Greene was given the command of Fort Mercer,

in Red Bank, New Jersey.
General Washington would
write to the young colonel:
"The post with which you are
entrusted is of the utmost importance to America. . . . The
whole defense of the Delaware
absolutely depends upon it,
and consequently all of the
enemy's hopes of keeping
Philadelphia and finally suc-
ceeding in the object of the
present campaign."

Christopher Greene
(1737–1781) by James Sullivan Lincoln (1863). (*Brown
University Portrait Collection*)

On October 11, 1777, soon
after the British occupation of
Philadelphia and victory at
Germantown, the 1st Rhode Island Regiment reached
the fort, where they discovered that there was much
work to do. The earthworks for the defense of Fort Mercer were only partially completed, and there seemed to
be, at least to one veteran, too few men to complete the
task. "The number of our men all told were short of five
hundred. Daily expecting an attack from the enemy, in
our unprepared and almost defenseless situation officers
and men without discrimination set to work with undi-
minished vigilance night and day to prepare a wing of the
Fort for defence."[8]

To further delay the completion, the men were also
required to perform garrison and fatigue duty at nearby
Fort Mifflin, a massive expanse of earthworks and artillery encampments thrown up on what the locals called
"Mud Island" across the Delaware from Fort Mercer and
within swimming distance of the Pennsylvania shore.
Each time a detachment of men were rowed from one

fort to the other, they came under bombardment from the enemy.

Washington was not unaware of their predicament. Colonel Greene had sent a letter asking for reinforcements, and in mid-October the general issued orders that the 2nd Rhode Island Regiment, under Colonel Israel Angell, be sent from the Grand Army to rejoin Greene and his troops at Fort Mercer. They departed on October 16 and began a grueling march of sixty miles with little food or rest before reaching the banks of the Delaware on the evening of October 18, 1777.

The 2nd Rhode Island Regiment had arrived just in time, for in less than twenty-four hours, Fort Mercer would come under attack. Twelve cannon, sending grapeshot and ball onto the ramparts, began bombarding the fort on October 19. The batteries of the Rhode Island regiments responded. Private Jeremiah Greenman with the 2nd Rhode Island Regiment would record in his diary, "the duty very hard indeed/ keep a continual fire on the Enemy & they on us."[9] He would record again on the 22nd that

> This morning are informed that a party of the Enemy crossed Cooper ferry last Evening and was on their way thro Haddenfield for this fort . . . / had scarce an opportunity to git into the Fort, before a Flag came to Colo. Green, who commanded the Fort, threatening to put the Garrison to (death) if he did not surrender it immediately, Colo. Green answered with disdain, that he would defend it 'till the last drop of his Blood-as soon as the Flag had returned they opined 7 field peaces & 2 Howitzers on the fort and played very smartly for about ten minutes then rushed on very Rash that even Success could not justify it's temerity.[10]

The Hessian Brigade, under command of Colonel Carl Emil Ulrich von Donop, was made up of three battalions, one infantry regiment, and a detachment of light infantry called Jagers, or "hunters," for their skill at marksmanship. The enemy advanced in two columns toward the regiments barricaded inside.

Greene had taken fifty rifle and artillery troops into an inner palisade and instructed them to wait for his orders. The Rhode Island soldiers amid the earthworks, under command of Lieutenant Colonel Jeremiah Olney, succeeded in breaking up one column with the accuracy of their fire, while the other column of Hessians advanced to a point inside of the outer barricades. Sure that they had entered the breastworks undefended, they sent up a cheer, only to be fired upon by Greene's hidden riflemen. The resulting volley swept the Hessians from the fort, and incurred heavy losses. The Germans lost twenty-five officers, with one hundred and twenty-seven killed, and roughly another two hundred men wounded.

Jeremiah Greenman would record that they spent the remainder of the day after the battle collecting the dead and wounded enemy. There were scores, however, and of that night, Captain Stephen Olney, who had delivered Col. Greene's message of defiance to the British delegate, would recall later, "I had charge of the guard that night / my Centrys were placed around the whole fort, that part evacuated was cover'd with dead, Dying and wounded Hessians, the groans and cries of the two latter were quite solitary musik."[11]

As mentioned, a number of free blacks had enlisted in the regiment, and one of the nation's earliest black historians, William Cooper Nell, writing his account while the nation was in the throes of civil war, attributed the victory in what became known as the Battle of Red Bank to their

"The Course of the Delaware River from Philadelphia to Chester, exhibiting the several works erected by the rebels to defend its passage, with the attacks made upon them by His Majesty's land & sea forces" by William Faden, 1778. Col. Donop's approach to Fort Mercer can

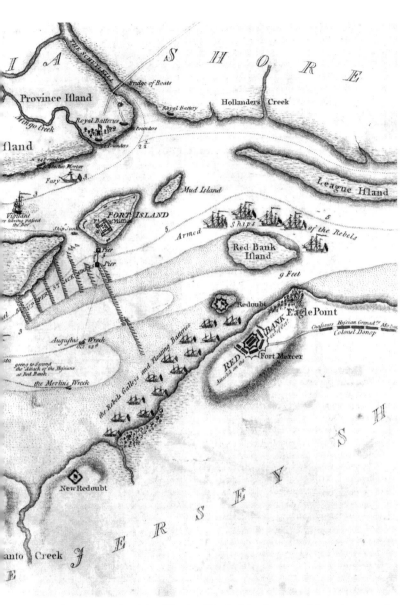

be seen on the right. The 1st Rhode Island was positioned among the earthworks around Fort Mercer, and the regiment successfully repelled the Hessian attackers in what became known as the Battle of Red Bank. (*Library of Congress*)

valor: "The glory of the defense of Red Bank, which has been pronounced one of the most heroic actions of the war, belonged in reality to black men."[12]

Colonel Christopher Greene's leadership was also lauded. Nell would write that the colonel had surrounded himself with a group of elite black soldiers who served as bodyguards. Greene was well known for his swordsmanship, and it was said that one never left his side. The colonel reportedly felt that a sword was far deadlier than a pistol in hand-to-hand combat.

While the news of the victory caused celebration, for the troops the victory was just one battle of a larger engagement, as British ships offshore and the Continental batteries on land exchanged heavy bombardment that left "four great ships in a blasé, floating on the Water / the Island & Main covered with Smoak & fire."[13] In November, both forts fell to the British.

As fall stretched into winter, the troops regrouped at Valley Forge. Harassed along the way by skirmishes with the redcoats, Greenman writes that his battalion arrived in mid-December at a place called Chester woods where they were to quarter for the winter, and over the course of several days "drawed axes to build huts for ye winter/ we began our huts / order'd to build them with logs 14 feet one way & 16 ye other / Continuing building our huts / nothing very Remarkable & C / mov'd in."[14]

The bleak landscape and cold nights continued to sap the strength of the Continental Army. Desertions had occurred throughout the summer, but increased dramatically after November 1. Ill fitted for winter and ill fed, those who did not desert often fell sick within the close confines of the quarters. The American army was now desperately thin of manpower, and plans were made to send officers back to recruit more troops to fill in the ranks.

That same year of 1777, Brigadier-General Varnum had written to General Washington, expressing his concern that "The two Battalions from the State of Rhode Island being small, and there being a necessity of the State's furnishing an additional number to make up their proportion in the Continental army, the field officers have represented to me the propriety of making one temporary battalion from the two, so that one entire corps of officers may repair to Rhode Island in order to receive and prepare recruits for the field."[15]

Varnum had another plan as well, which would prove to be as revolutionary as the war against Great Britain.

2

From Slaves to Soldiers

Varnum's plan, put forward to General Washington, was that rather than just a few blacks being integrated into a handful of regiments, that an entirely black regiment be raised in Rhode Island. The commander wrote confidently, "It is imagined that a battalion of Negroes may be easily raised there. Should that measure be adopted or recruits obtained under any other principle, the service will be advanced."[1]

Written in his headquarters where he wintered and entertained at Valley Forge, Varnum's proposal was in response to the British offer of freedom for slaves who chose to escape their masters and became loyalists. Such an idea had been introduced by black activists to tory leaders in Boston while that city lay under siege, but the official proclamation given by Virginia governor Lord Dunmore in November 1775 had caused a tide of blacks to flood the British fort in Williamsburg, with wives, children, and grandmothers in tow.[2]

Things were rather different in the north. Reportedly alarmed to find so many armed African Americans when he arrived in Boston to take command,[3] Washington first forbade black men to enlist in the Continental troops, or the main army, but had to grudgingly permit those free blacks who had already enrolled in local militias to remain, and to allow blacks to be embedded within the Continental Army, in the months that followed Dunmore's proclamation.[4]

There is strong evidence that Rhode Island towns may have enacted such measures prior to Varnum's proposal. Of the British troops ensconced in Newport, Major Frederick MacKenzie would write in his diary on June 30, 1777: "Two Negroes who came over from Narragansett this day." The black men told the British command that the Colony was in "confusion," that money in one county was worthless in the next, and that "provisions are scarce and dear, and very little corn to be had. And that they find it so difficult to raise men for the Continental Army that they enlist negroes, for whom their owners receive a bounty of 180 dollars, and half their pay, and the Negroe gets the other half, and the promise of freedom at the end of three years."[5]

One of these recruits may have been Isaac Howland, who was listed as "able to serve" in 1777, but registered with the Sons of the American Revolution as "a negroe servant for officer." Officers in the Continental Army were assigned "waiters," who served as personal assistants during their enlistment. Sampson or Samuel Oakman served as a waiter to General Nathanael Greene, and a young black soldier named Aaron Snow served as the same to Lieutenant Joseph Wheaton.

Murray Lippit's master was an officer in the Continental Army, and he continued to serve as his personal servant during the war. Other slaves who served with their masters included Amistus Weeden and Nathaniel West. A list in the hand of Colonel Christopher Greene records the "Return of the men's names who are free and inlisted for the term of 2 years in the 2nd company of foot Commanded by Lieut. Burlingame, Dec. 1779":

1. Thomas Taylor January 1777
2. George Popple April 1777
3. James Moses Feb. 1777
4. John Dunbar – Private (?) 1777
5. Dick (Richard) Allen May 22, 1777
6. Caesar Sabins (?) 1777

All of these men, as indicated, enlisted in 1777, some more than a year before the enactment of the Assembly's resolution allowing blacks into the Continental Army.

Greene's documents also contain a list of thirty-three free blacks enlisted in the Continental Line.[6] Also in 1777, a Hessian officer noted a prevalence of blacks among the Continental troops, writing that "You never see a regiment in which there are not negroes, and there are well-built, strong, husky fellows among them."[7]

In fact, these men also appear on the muster for the 1st Rhode Island Regiment in 1778, as they were transferred from the 2nd Rhode Island to help form the "black regiment." But not all the black men witnessed among the troops were soldiers.

Historian Ira Berlin argues that many slaves seized the opportunity, in whatever way they could, for the chance of becoming free: "Black men leveraged their freedom as soldiers. But others—women as well as men—likewise secured their liberty on the battlefield, even if they never picked up a musket. Rather, they traded their labor working as teamsters, boatmen, seamstresses, and domestics, doing much of the dirty work of war in exchange for freedom."[8]

It may be that slaves taken into battalions prior to the forming of the 1st Rhode Island Regiment were put into service as personal servants, or tasked with menial labor for the army, such as collecting wood or cleaning the camp. But the number of black men in Rhode Island allowed for the possibility of some being trained as infantry troops, and even the raising of an entire regiment of black soldiers.

As early as 1708, the city of Newport was well populated with "men of color," both free and enslaved. Many free blacks signed aboard vessels, but there were plenty of other opportunities in commercial trades. The census of that year found that there were 426 black servants in the colony, many of these undoubtedly in the homes of the port city and in the homes of the Narragansett Planters. Providence was also a slave-holding community, but on a smaller scale until mid-century.

In his landmark work, *The Negro in Colonial New England*, historian Lorenzo Johnston Greene noted that "Negroes were identified with every phase of New England's economy and, as a consequence, slave labor was highly diversified. The very character of New England's economic development rendered inevitable, a variety of slave occupations. . . . These would include farming, lumbering, trading, fishing, whaling, manufacturing, and privateering."[9]

In Rhode Island, the largest slave owner would aspire to create a southern sized plantation in the seaside town of Newport. Abraham Redwood owned a total of 238 slaves on his family plantation in Antigua at the height of

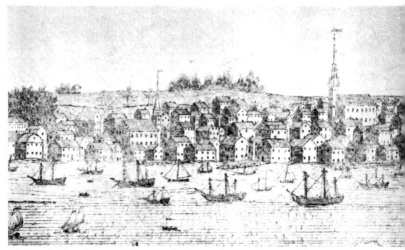

"A South West View of Newport," drawn shortly after the American Revolution. (*New York Public Library*)

his costly effort in 1766, though the slave merchant never saw his Newport plantation reach that population, and is now better remembered for his philanthropy, and the library in the city that bears his name.[10] The greatest concentration of slaves would come to be in South Kingstown, or the "Narragansett Country." "Upon these extensive acres," Greene wrote, "there developed a landed aristocracy, popularly known as the 'Narragansett Planters,' a group without a counterpart in New England, but possessing many of the characteristics of the manorial lords of New York or the plantation Barons of the South."[11]

Robert Hazard, a descendant of one planter family, whose recollections would be famously published at the close of the nineteenth century, would equate his ancestors with the landed gentry in England, for along the southern coast of Narragansett Bay, men and women rode in their best finery on the sure-footed Narragansett Pac-

ers along "the bridal path that led from one great farm to another . . . the ladies in their camblitt cloaks, and the gentlemen in broadcloth and britches, with silver shoe and knee buckles." But while Hazard wrote wistfully of the early farms on which his ancestors aspired to be like English squires, he plainly stated that these great farms all were worked "with slave labor, either indian, or negro, or both."[12]

The majority of those slaves that worked in the Narragansett Country worked on large dairy farms, an early and long-standing product of the farms was "good Rhode Island cheese." Others worked in raising vegetable and tobacco crops or herding the large number of sheep on the estates. While some farms in the country were about three hundred acres, the Updikes at Smith's Castle, and the farms of the Stantons, Hazards, Champlins, Robinsons, Gardiners, and Potters extended over several thousand acres.[13]

Wilkins Updike would elaborate on the planter's lifestyle afforded by the slave labor imported to Rhode Island:

> "This state of society supported by slavery would produce festivity and dissipation, the natural result of wealth and leisure. Excursions to Hartford to luxuriate on *bloated* salmon were the annual indulgences of May. Pace(r) races on the beach for the prize of a silver tankard and roasts of shelled and scaled fish were the social indulgences of summer. When autumn arrived, the *corn husking* festivals commenced. Invitations were extended to all those proprietors . . . and in return the invited guests sent their slaves to aid the host by their services."[14]

The 1749 census shows that there were 3,077 blacks in Rhode Island, or 9.3 percent of the total population. The population of blacks would continue to increase until about 1755 when one of every three persons in South Kingstown was black.

By comparison, though the plantations in the southern colonies would later become much larger, these early southern plantations were much like those in Rhode Island. As historian Peter Charles Hoffer explains, "Carolina planters grew rice in the 1690s, but it did not become the colony's major crop until the 1720s. The arrival from Africa of a new variety of rice seed, joined with the skills of blacks from parts of Africa familiar with rice cultivation, turned what had seemed at first an unprofitable experiment . . . into a gold mine."[15]

South Carolina's slave population had grown to 2.6 slaves for every white person by 1740, a ratio that was similar to other southern colonies. With this increase in the slave population came a slew of measures to control the slaves in both the southern and northern colonies. Vir-

ginia laws viewed slaves gathering for funerals or "feasts"
to be "of dangerous consequence" and forbade then from
bringing firearms to such gatherings. South Carolina's
Slave Code of 1740 declared that any attempt or threat
by a slave to strike a white person was "a serious offense."[16]

In 1750, Rhode Island passed a law barring households
from entertaining black or indigenous servants after 9 in
the evening. In addition, during those hours of legal entertainment, the host was obligated to restrain their
guests from any "dancing, gaming, or any other diversion
whatever." The offending householder faced a fine of £50
and imprisonment for a month for any violation. The law
was even harsher on those free indigenous, blacks, and
mulattoes in Rhode Island communities. If these citizens
were found guilty of giving said "entertainment" to a
slave, they lost their house to the town and were expelled
from the community. Free people of color in Rhode Island were often easily adapted into the smaller towns,
having usually been manumitted by the death of their
owner, and thus a familiar, and often elderly face in the
community. Those younger free blacks who set out to be
an apprentice or laborer in adjoining or far-flung towns
found themselves constantly questioned and having to
prove their freedom, as well as their livelihood, if they
were not to be "warned out" of a community.

In most Rhode Island communities, slaves could not
own a pig or cow or any other livestock. A slave could not
purchase any merchandise without permission of his master. From early on, Rhode Island exhibited some of the
strictest punishments for those who aided runaway slaves.
In an effort to curb the flight of slaves from the colony,
ferrymen were fined for giving a ride to any indigenous
or black person who failed to show a letter of intent from

their master. In addition, the offending ferryman was obligated to compensate the master of the slave he had transported for all costs and charges received during the period of his loss.

Perhaps most degrading to the slave and indentured servants was the way in which their masters and the state viewed them as property. Slaves were assessed as any other property and taxed accordingly by the colony. A typical assessment of 1707 classifies the slaves with the domestic animals of each household, determining that males over fourteen were to be valued at £20 each, while females over fourteen were valued at £15. In this manner, slaves were deemed "ratable property" though Massachusetts distinguished between Negro, Indian, and mulatto slaves and indentured domestic servants of the same races, which were to be rated as polls, individually.[17]

Rhode Island inventories of property include slaves on the list with houses, barns, mill buildings, wharves, windmills, and accounts drawing interest. Among the items in the extensive inventory of Samuell Winsor's "Old dwelling house" after his death in September 1715, was a servant boy valued at £10. After Providence mariner John Dexter died in June 1716, an inventory of his estate included over 150 pounds of molasses in barrels, sundry articles of clothing, "10 books, 2 wigs . . . 2 gold rings," and the most valuable of his possessions, the "negroe woman and a negroe boy," assessed at £60 together. The executors in Providence assessing John Hause's estate in December 1726 placed his "negro woman" on the list between Hause's "sorrild horse" and his bedpan.

While an old law on the books prevented owners from bequeathing or selling slaves from their households, this was largely ignored, and the will of Robert Hazard of Newport is testimony to the manner in which slaves were "inherited" from one family member to another. Hazard's will reads in part: "I give to my beloved wife Sarah, my mulatto woman called Lydia, and four cows . . . to my daughter Sarah . . . two feather beds . . . one bay mare, also my negro woman Bell, or Isabel . . . to my son Jonathan, my negro man Newport . . . also mulatto boy Dick."[18] Hazard also bequeathed two black female children, one named Phillis to his wife, the other named Phebe to his daughter. The document does not state the children's ages, or to whom they were born among the servants.

Indentured servants could also be passed among a family after the death of their owner. Such was the case with the "Indian servant girl" of Samuel Gorton in Cranston, who, the council noted, still had "2 years and 10 months to serve." Among the items in Gorton's inventory was a "chase bed for the Indian servant."[19]

Slaves of those masters who died intestate in the early colonial period were confiscated and sold off "for the betterment of the community." On the death of John Mathewson in September 1718, his female slave became the property of the town of Providence. The same occurred for the female slave of John Angell four years later. Later in the century the practice began to change. As Lorenzo Greene noted, "Not until the eve of open hostilities with Great Britain were negroes . . . who became town property given their freedom." When Jacob Shoemaker died intestate in 1774, he left six blacks, four of them infants who then became the property of the town of Providence. Fully embroiled in the struggle for liberty, the town's fathers could not in good conscience sell the slaves as had been previously done. In the town meeting, they declared it "unbecoming to the character of freemen to enslave the said negroes." The town surrendered any claims to the slaves as property. The adult slaves were placed under the care of the town and the children bound over to service.[20]

This did not mean, however, that the citizens of Providence, or any other city within the colonies were prepared to arm those slaves or free their black men, even as they urged other citizens to join the militias forming in many communities. This was not always the case. As early as 1652, the colony of Massachusetts had required that all blacks and Native Americans who quartered with or were servants of citizens to undergo military training. By the end of the century, responding to the fear of uprisings, Massachusetts and Connecticut had reversed course, and indeed, slaves and indigenous people were barred from military service.

WHILE GREAT BRITAIN'S COLONIES HAD LARGELY SHUNNED those indigenous and black men from duty, the mother country and its European enemies used indigenous tribes and slaves to prop up the campaigns of faltering empires throughout much of the eighteenth century. The Carolinas in North America were the first to be affected. In what became known as the Yamasee War, Carolina planters reluctantly impressed their slaves into service against the Yamasee Indians who had ambushed a band of English authorities sent to negotiate with them in April 1715. News of the attack spread among neighboring indigenous nations, and South Carolina soon found itself under assault, with Southeastern Indian warriors burning many of the colony's plantations and threatening Charlestown within a few months of the initial attack. Even with the plantation city under imminent threat, many of the Carolina planters were uneasy at arming the slaves for fear that once armed, they "might become our masters."[21] Despite these concerns, by summer of that year, a force of "100 white men and 100 Negroes and Indians" were impressed under command of Governor Charles Craven. While these forces proved successful, there were also slaves, "many having run away from their masters already," who aligned themselves with enemy nations and joined in the raids on plantations.

The news of an uprising and murder of forty whites in the Danish Caribbean sent shock waves through the colonies. Unrest and desertions from Barbados and Jamaica were also unsettling events, and as the slave population continued to grow in the North American colonies, fears of an uprising or mass desertion began to plague plantation owners.

In November 1733, an edict from the Spanish ruler had been read in St. Augustine harbor, within hearing distance of those aboard slave ships bound for the colonies, which promised "Liberty and protection to all slaves that deserted to his realm."[22] In fact, slaves had been fleeing southward from the Carolinas for some time, and those fit to serve had been integrated into Spanish military units, where they were eager to wage war on their former owners. In the wake of the Spanish edict, some slave owners faced "dayly desertion," which began to affect the production on the plantations. As difficulties increased in the Caribbean, plantation owners from the islands removed themselves and their slaves to the Carolinas. This exodus to North America added to the tension in the region. Those fears found fruition in September 1739 when a mass uprising of slaves occurred in South Carolina, known as the Stono Rebellion.

South Carolina law at that time required planters to provide slaves for repairing roads, removing silt from waterways, and digging drainage ditches, among other tasks of what today we would call public works projects. Such a project was approved along the Stono River in the summer of 1739. The parish commissioner duly collected about two dozen slaves from the nearby plantations, many of them recently arrived from the Kongo region of southwestern Africa. These slaves faced weeks of digging ditches through snake-and insect-infected wetlands to meet the commissioner's deadline before the heavy rains that would come in the fall.

The conventional histories tell us that these men were warriors, and planned the revolt to escape and find refuge in Florida. More recently, historian Peter Charles Hoffer has challenged that assumption, arguing that their actions of revolt were spontaneous, and borne of more recent frustration than the result of a well-thought-out plan.

As the ditch crew finished work around sundown on September 8, 1739, they found themselves alone and unsupervised. The overseer had left before darkness fell, and the men knew they would gather at the same place the next morning, even though it was the Sabbath day. Slaves were generally given the Sabbath off as a day of rest, but the commissioner had deemed that the digging continue regardless of the day or weather, until the ditches were completed. As Hoffer writes, "Bone tired, thirsty, and hungry, they griped in the way that manual laborers do at the end of the workday. There was no plan to raise the countryside in rebellion, no grand scheme to undo slavery, no plot to run riot. The grumbling simply got worse, gaining focus and momentum."[23]

Some of the crew made their way to Hutchinson's, a nearby store known well to the diggers. As darkness had descended, their intent was likely to plunder the store of food and drink. When they found two men, laborer Robert Bathurst and highway commissioner John Gibbs, inside, a confrontation ensued. The whites were murdered within minutes, and in the ensuing chaos, some of the crew grabbed guns and ammunition while others fled back to their plantations. "Faced with the enormity of their unplanned actions, some of the slaves probably followed the lead of other members of the crew who had earlier vanished, reappearing in the quarters as though nothing had happened. . . . But those slaves who returned to their quarters after the murders spread the word of the murders among others in nearby houses, and no doubt revealed as well that some of the drain crew . . . had moved on in their thinking to a more general, and violent, form of resistance."[24]

Those who remained in the store, now driven by desperation and fear, made their way to Godfrey's Landing, likely to make their escape, but were again confronted, and the slaves killed everyone in the house. They moved on through the county, seemingly randomly, as if in a drunken rage, breaking into another home and killing the inhabitants, then stopped at another house occupied by a slave named Wells, who had hid his owners and managed to persuade the band of armed men to leave them unharmed. Throughout the night the remnants of the band moved through the countryside along the river, plundering the houses and killing those inside the houses they passed on the Pon Pon Road. In all, twenty-one persons were murdered.

The reaction by authorities was swift. Members of the local militia were called out of church services the following morning and gathered in the village of Willtown with militia from other towns, amid rumors that the rebellious slaves had gathered others with them, marching along the Pon Pon Road to the beat of a drum. The men could only imagine that these slaves, too, were now armed as well.

By that afternoon the militia had tracked the rebellious slaves and their followers to a field about fifteen miles from Wallace Creek. They heard the singing and dancing before they reached the large field in which William Stephens witnessed the gathering, "where they were dancing, being most of them drunk with the liquors they found in the stores." The men of the Willtown militia dismounted and crept to the edge of the field where they hastily formed a line, raised their rifles, and fired a first volley. Other militia were close on their heels and fired a second volley into the panicked gathering. The official report would record that "about 40 negroes were killed," though this was apparently the total killed during the first assault, as well as the day after, spent pursuing those who had fled into the woods. Many others who had returned to the plantations were summarily taken out and shot per their master's order.[25]

In the aftermath of the killings, newspapers far and wide across the country held readers spellbound with reports of the uprising. "The Great Stono River Slave Rebellion," as it was called, would be the first in a series of highly publicized uprisings and killings on plantations that fed fears of a massive uprising in the coming decades.

By the mid-1750s, Spanish pirates were continually harassing ships from the colonies, and the governors of Virginia and Georgia were pleading with Britain to place more redcoats on the streets. Virginia governor Robert Dinwiddle lamented that the twin fears of foreign invasion and slave uprising had plagued his colony for nearly a century.[26]

Just prior to the outbreak of the French and Indian War in 1756, a report on the status of the New York–New Jersey region voiced concern of "too great (an) intimacy between the negro slaves and the French neutrals in the Province."[27] The fear was that with so many men off to fight the French, the sympathizers might incite the slaves to insurrection. The French had motivated their native allies to assist their cause with lavish presents and promises of new treaties. Britain had followed the same path in using the escaped slaves and the indigenous people of their New England colonies.

It was a costly war, but one in which Great Britain retained its hold on North America and expelled the threats from France and Spain alike. Not lost within the analysis of this victory was that Britain had enlisted enslaved African men and others in the New York militia to accompany the redcoats in the far-flung skirmishes against the French and their indigenous allies. One such soldier was Henry Brown. A report in the *Providence Journal* in November 1822 stated that Brown was still living at the age of 125 in Pennsylvania. The newspaper reported that Brown had been born in 1696 to a Negro father, and an Indian mother. He had been a slave for seventy years, and now had been a freeman for fifty-eight. Henry Brown was "a soldier at Braddock's defeat in 1755, then aged 59."[28]

Still, on the eve of the revolution, the colonies were deeply divided on the issue of allowing black slaves, indigenous men, and indentured servants of mixed races into local militias. In the midst of war, even Georgia had debated enlisting "Negroes that may be trusted with arms."[29]

One loyalist however, believed that all sorts of outsiders, from convicts to servants, Indians, and slaves could be mustered for the defense of the state. John Murray, the Earl of Dunmore, was a Scottish aristocrat who had been assigned as governor of New York before being reassigned amid much protest to Virginia. Though the posting was a step up from his duties in New York, he and his wife had made a home there, along with friends and business contacts. He was a colorful, headstrong politician, nearly always bucking or delaying orders from Whitehall. Nonetheless, Dunmore took the post as ordered, and as tensions between the colonies and Great Britain mounted, he was determined to do all he could to quell the impending rebellion.

In July 1775, the governor was taking a rest at his hunting lodge on the York River, just a few miles from Williamsburg. During a meal on July 11, Dunmore's slaves on the grounds noticed a large body of armed men marching toward the lodge. These were the Hanover County volunteers, the local militia who had threatened Dunmore several months earlier for his "confiscation" of gunpowder from the Williamsburg magazine. The slaves alerted the governor and he escaped minutes before he would have been captured. As biographer James Corbett David writes, "From that point forward, black Americans were among Dunmore's most important allies."[30]

Throughout that summer, slaves and indentured servants reached out to Dunmore. One slave even offered to guard the Governor's Palace in exchange for freedom. By November, Dunmore had tested the political waters and found them warming to the idea of arming slaves for the loyalist cause. On the 15th, he issued a far-reaching proclamation, which declared that "All indentured Servants, Negroes, or others (appertaining to the Rebels) free, that are able and willing to bear Arms, they joining his Majesty's troops, as soon as they may be for the more speedily reducing this Colony to a proper Sense of their Duty."[31]

In little more than a month, Dunmore's proclamation had brought about the escape of more than two hundred

slaves. It is estimated that in all, more than 1,000 and perhaps as many as 1,500 escaped slaves reached the governor's harbor of safety. Those able-bodied men were soon
enlisted in "Dunmore's Ethiopian Regiment" and paid
monthly wages. White officers commanded the regiment.
Ultimately, it is estimated that tens of thousands of blacks
fled slavery in those southern states and found refuge
within British-held territory.

Such seems not to have been the case, however, in the
north, where few slaves or free blacks turned themselves
over to the protection of British authorities. Some local
historians have argued that a considerable number of
blacks fled their masters while the British occupied Newport, but the diary of Major Frederick MacKenzie clearly
states the difficulty the army faced in persuading blacks
to join them: "The Negroes on this Island have been in-
vited to join the King's Troops, and have been promised
pay and provisions; but very few of them having come in,
Orders were given to bring in all those who are capable
of any service, as they are much wanted as drivers, and
for other services."[32]

Indeed, one slave named Quaco, who had been sold
by his master in Newport to a British officer and who
found the service in a British regiment "extremely disagreeable to him," fled from the island and did "place
himself under the protection of this government; and did,
by the information he then gave, render great and essential service to this state and the public in general." The
State Assembly in 1782 declared him "manumitted and
absolved from all ties of bondage and slavery"[33] for his
service, refuting the claims of his master for his return.

Another slave named Jehu Grant suspected that his
master Elihu Champlen of Narragansett "in a secret manner furnished the enemy when shipping lay nearby with

sheep, cattle, cheese, etc." When the neighbors began to suspect as well, and branded Champlen a tory, Grant feared his master would turn him over with the other goods to a British ship, and fled "sometime in August 1777."[34]

He made his way to Danbury, Connecticut, where Grant enlisted with a regiment under Capt. Giles Gailor for eighteen months. He worked as a teamster, drawing provisions with a team of horses and wagon for three or four months until winter. He was also a servant to "wagon-master general" John Skidmore, and "carried the said General Skidmore's baggage and continued with him and the said troops as his wagoneer" to the "Highlands" above the Hudson River and the British lines.[35]

During this same period, a British coaster foraging the shoreline came upon a black man fishing off the spindle beyond Watch Hill in Westerly, Rhode Island, and took him prisoner. This man, named Vester, was well known in his community as "a man of great stature and strength," capable of lifting "a tierce of molasses, or carry seven bushels of salt," and a powerful swimmer, whose habit was to swim to the spindle at low tide and fish until driven by the flood tide to return to Watch Hill.

Upon his capture, Vester was taken to Fishers Island and held as a slave, tasked with heavy labor for the British use of the island as a supply depot for the mainland forces. He soon determined to make his escape and one night during the season of the ebb tide, he "plunged into the Sound, swam out into the current, and, resting as a floater, was borne by the tide opposite Watch Hill, when resuming his great power as a swimmer, he safely reached the shore, and returned home."[36]

The historian includes the tale in the town's history "as it was told," with a skeptical eye, and perhaps rightly so, but the story itself, if only legend among locals, may shed greater light on the defiant spirit held by many free blacks in the colony toward British rule.[37]

IN THE WINTER OF 1777, VARNUM'S PROPOSAL FOR AN ALL-black regiment of manumitted slaves caught the eye of the Continental Army's commander-in-chief. It was a compelling argument for recruitment, and in December of that year, facing a lean winter at Valley Forge, and the loss of nearly half his army as their time of service expired, Washington passed the letter onto Rhode Island's governor Nicholas Cooke with a note, which read in part: "Enclosed you will find a copy of a letter from General Varnum to me upon the means which might be adopted for completing the Rhode Island troops to their full proportion in the Continental army. . . . I have nothing to say in addition . . . on this important subject, but to desire that you will give the officers employed in this business all the assistance in your power."[38]

The proposal was duly placed before the General Assembly, though not without opposition. Many slaveholders in Rhode Island had adopted the fear, with the news of violence in the southern colonies and of revolts on islands long held by those fading empires, that arming former slaves would lead to insurrections on many of the larger "plantations" in the colony. Despite these protests, the General Assembly was more inclined to favor General Washington's request, but in doing so, also opened the door for slave owners to choose which among their slaves could enlist. In February 1778, the Rhode Island General Assembly issued the proclamation that "every able bodied negro, mulatto, or Indian man slave in this state may inlist into either of the said two battalions to serve during the continuance of the war with Great Britain; that every slave so inlisting shall be entitled to, and receive all the bounties, wages, and encouragements allowed by the Continental Congress . . . that every slave inlisting shall, upon passing muster before Colonel Christopher Greene, be immediately discharged from the service of his master or mistress, and be absolutely FREE, as though he had never been incumbered with any kind of servitude or slavery."[39]

The state of Rhode Island would pay each owner the assessed value of each slave who had passed muster "a sum according to his worth, not exceeding one hundred and twenty pounds for the most valuable slave and in proportion for a slave of less value."

Governor Cooke wrote to General Washington, laying out the state's plan in response to his request. "The number of slaves in this state is not great; but it is generally thought that three hundred, and upwards, will be enlisted."[40]

A commission of five men was appointed to value each slave after they had passed muster, and enlistments began. Within weeks, eighty-eight slaves had signed on for the regiment, the first said to be Cuff Greene, a slave in the service of the governor's son, James Greene.[41]

Bounty receipts from North Providence in the collection of the Rhode Island Historical Society Library, show that Jabez Whipple, one of the recruitment officers, paid slave owners a bounty of sixty-five dollars a man, as the receipt of Admiral Esek Hopkins, who owned an estate in the town illustrates: "Received of Jabez Whipple the sum of sixty-five dollars in Consideration there of I promise that my Negro Loser Shall Serve As a faithful soldier in Capt. Ebenezer Jenckes Company in Cornall John Matthewson ('s) Regiment in the Room of John Cumstock who Refuses to bear arms in the expedition now forming Against Newport."

Still, there were dissenters amid the Assembly who continued their arguments that there were scarce enough able-bodied black men to form a regiment, that the owners of said slaves would argue about compensation, and the expense was therefore far greater than to enlist another regiment of white soldiers. Six dissenters from the vote expressed the view that such a regiment would be looked upon with contempt by the troops from other colonies, and that the state itself, would be given the reputation of having to purchase "a band of slaves to defend the Rights and Liberties of the country." Furthermore, they wrote, such an act would be "wholly inconsistent with those principles of liberty and constitutional government, for which we are so ardently contending, . . . and would also give occasion to our enemies to suspect that we are not able to procure our own people to oppose them in the field."[42]

Despite the argument from these legislators, some slave owners were not opposed to sending slaves as "substitutes" for themselves, or for a family member who had been listed as eligible to serve by the town to fill the quota for enlistment. Indeed this was occurring in other New England towns as well, and at times, crossed state lines. Elkanah Watson of Plymouth furnished his slave Dolphin for thirty days service in Rhode Island in September 1777.[43] This seems also to have been the practice among the remaining Narragansett Planters, as records show that Caesar Babcock was a "slave and substitute" for Hezekiah Babcock, as was London Hazard for a relative of his master Godfrey Hazard.[44] William Wanton of Tiverton also served as a substitute for his master.[45] In

North Kingstown, Sheriff Beriah Brown sent his slave
Joseph as a substitute for his son Christopher.[46]

A good number of slaves came from these northern
plantations, including three from the Updike plantation,
seven from Champlin's, six from the Gardiners, five from
the Hazard farm, two from the Robinson's estate, and two
from the Watson Farm in South County. In total, thirty-
two slaves came from this county alone.[47]

Bowing to pressure from the opposition, the Assembly
passed a resolution in May, amending the law to a temporary measure: "Whereas by an act of this Assembly
negro, mullatto, and *Indian* slaves belonging to the inhabitants of this state are permitted to enlist into the Continental Battalions ordered to be raised by this State . . .
and whereas it is necessary for answering the purposes intended by the said act that the same should be temporary;
it is therefore voted and resolved, that no *negro, mulatto*,
or *Indian* slave be permitted to enlist into said battalions
from and after the tenth day of June next, and that the
said act expire and be no longer in force."

After the success of the appeal, only another forty-four
slaves enlisted with the regiment. The official register of
the 1st Rhode Island Regiment lists two hundred and
twenty-five men, one hundred forty of which were listed
as being "negro, mulatto, or mustee." No doubt, some
listed beneath this latter category were indigenous men
of the Narragansett, and other tribes. As later documents
show, indigenous men from southern New England
would remain part of the regiment throughout the war.

For narragansett men, their decision to join the
Continental Army came amidst a time of turmoil within
their tribe. One hundred years after King Philip's War and

the Great Swamp Massacre, many of the remaining indigenous people were enslaved, indentured, or displaced
from their traditional villages. Some had moved to Brothertown, New York, as well as to other tribal communities
around the region. One Brothertown historian found that
a good number of Narragansett men of the community
served in the war, including James Niles, a descendant of
the preacher Samuel.[48] Abraham Simons enlisted in the
6th Connecticut Regiment, with cousins Emmanuel and
James. John Skeesuck returned to Rhode Island and enlisted in Col. John Topham's regiment.

Those remaining in their homeland were being
pushed into less desirable locations. Their way of life as
they had known it was irrevocably changed. The tribe
had survived through one hundred and fifty years of broken treaties, colonization, genocide, displacement, the attempted cultural assimilation of their people, as well as
enslavement and the erasure of their indigenous identity,
through town records and the first Eurocentric histories
of the region.

Survival was utmost in mind. Individual, familial, clan,
community, tribal, and intertribal concerns were at the
forefront of the decision to join the army. Some, as historian Colin G. Calloway speculates, may have believed
that serving in the war would provide an opportunity to
obtain freedoms they had not been given before. In addition, indigenous people have a long history of honor
and respect for warriors. Many Native American communities had and have warrior societies that are designed
with ceremony throughout. Both male and female warriors participated in ceremony at the commencement of
the conflict to conduct themselves with honor, respect,
and dignity.

In November 1940, Princess Redwing, of Narragansett and Wampanoag descent and an advocate of indigenous rights for her people and American Indians throughout southern New England, was asked to address the Woonsocket Chapter of the Daughters of the American Revolution. In her remarks, she spoke of those traditions among the indigenous peoples of southern New England, and specifically noted that the Narragansett people had traditionally been taught that "This is the land of their fathers and mothers. We also teach them to sing from their souls and 'love the rocks and rills, thy woods and templed hills', this is their own, their native land."[49]

Portrait of an indigenous soldier of the 1st Rhode Island Regiment by Allan Archanbeault. (*Courtesy of the Rhode Island Society of the Sons of the American Revolution*)

Oral history states that Narragansett men joined the war for freedom, for empowerment, for warrior pride, to protect their families, communities, way of life, homelands, and to provide hope for future generations. Perhaps with a century of conflict with the English in mind, those indigenous people, and both free blacks and slaves who enlisted in the Continental Army felt that with the shared experience of throwing off the yoke of British rule over the colonies, such freedoms that belonged to every man might be given to them.

Those indigenous men who bore the surname of Hazard, Brown, Champlin, or Gardiner, among other Euro-American names; were almost certainly the indentured servants or slaves of those masters who added their own name of ownership to the indigenous man. Many more, who appear on the 1777 military census, were individuals who enlisted of their own accord. Chair of the National Algonquian Indian Council Nancy Brown-Garcia writes:

> There were Indians who were free and others who were indentured, seeking freedom, but most were free and lived on poor reservations and sought the good possibilities being a soldier who served and survived could bring: freedom, honor, and a war pension when older. These opportunities made a poor, bored reservation warrior willing to go to war. From the beginning Narragansett warriors chose battle rather than a bleak existence. When Canonchet and his father[50] were asked how they liked death/and or war, they both preferred death while their hearts were strong, as opposed to old age when their hearts had grown soft.[51]

There is little record from journals on how the common soldiers already embedded with the regiment felt about the new recruits. Pvt. Jeremiah Greenman would record on March 27, 1778, that "this morn we peraded our Slaves for to march to Grinnage."[52] Greenman's use of the word "slaves" may reflect the common foot soldiers' belief that these men were not yet proven, nor were they free until they had served their time.

The recruits were marched into Massachusetts, back across the border to Rhode Island, down to South County, back to Providence, and returned to East Greenwich ("Grinage," in Greenman's journal) within a matter of sixteen days. On that cloudy Tuesday in March, Greenman would record that the troops were "Continuing in Grinage Exersis(ing) our Recrutes . . . / in ye after part of the day turn'd out our black (troops) / rec'd sum orders picked out a guard of 20 men & a sub. then marched down to Quidneset ware we made a guard house (out) of a dweling house half a mile from ye Shore ware we set 5 Sentinals / at day Light took off our Sentinals / march(t) up to Grinag."[53]

And so it went, through a wet spring, pushing on through May to reach Valley Forge, where they found it "very sickly in camp," likely due to it being "very raw & cold for the time of year." They remained there for ten days before striking out again, marching an average of four to seven miles a day, encamping in places such as "Newbriton, Amwell, Crambury," and "Englishtown."

No matter where they settled word of enemy movement would come, and the troops would again strike camp and march, pressing on toward the day when the inevitable battle would come.

3

Battles, Blood,
and Brotherhood

THE FARMERS, LABORERS, INDIGENOUS MEN, INDENTURED
servants, and former slaves of the 1st Rhode Island
Regiment would see their first action during the Battle
of Rhode Island on August 29, 1778.

The British had occupied the island of Newport almost from the beginning of hostilities, securing the island
on December 8, 1776, but it was never an easy occupation. The redcoats were harassed by skirmishes with
small parties of the enemy bent on raids and disruption,
as well as the kidnapping of their General Prescott at a
farm in Middletown. Their redoubts were fired upon routinely by passing privateers, and a host of other difficulties beset the British.

A summons to the inhabitants of neighboring
Portsmouth in September 1777 to assemble and assist

with the building of redoubts brought out only seventeen people. Major Frederick MacKenzie explained in his diary, "The Majority of the Inhabitants being Quakers, they informed the General that it was contrary to their principles to assist, in any manner in matters of War, and that therefore they could not appear."[1]

Later that same month, the major would write of the desertions plaguing the troops: "It is a matter of consequence, and should be attended to, as above 25 British Soldiers have deserted from three Battalions since the 1st of June last." MacKenzie believed that it was inhabitants of the island who were helping these deserters "with the means of going off from the S.E. part of the Island, which is seldom visited by any of our parties or patroles, and is very little frequented."[2] It would not be until late February 1778, that a captured deserter would be hung for his offense, an example MacKenzie thought "much wanted on this Island in order to deter the soldiers from committing a crime, which, although it is in these times one of the greatest a soldier can commit, has been too prevalent of late."[3]

The weather and accompanying sickness were also concerns. More than one sentry froze to death at his post that winter, and one apparently trying to return was found dead on the road the next morning.

By April, with the troops on the island still waiting for General Howe's fleet to appear, MacKenzie would worriedly write, "General Pigot has received certain intelligence that Mr. Sullivan is daily expected at Providence to take the Command of the Rebel troops in this Neighborhood; and as he is an enterprising spirited fellow, it is likely he will succeed in his endeavors to collect a sufficient body of men to enable him to make some attempt on this Island before we receive any reinforcement, or have further time to strengthen our position."[4]

From then on, into the summer, it was a waiting game as both sides viewed the other's preparations, and engaged in the occasional skirmish with rebels who landed on the island with the intent of raiding homes or engaging sentries.

After a morning of "Heavy rain, with Thunder & Lightening" on July 25, MacKenzie would note, "About 9 this morning a fleet of large ships appeared to the S.E. standing for the harbour, and they were soon discovered to be French; and about 12 they came too of the S. end of the Island."

This arrival of the French fleet would mark the beginning of the Rhode Island campaign; the French besieged the British fortifications with cannon fire and sent raiding parties onto the island, both to obtain supplies, as well as keep the British guessing as to the landing point of the impending attack to wrest back the island.

When the full measure of the fleet, which consisted of twelve ships of the line, four frigates, and four transports carrying nearly 4,000 soldiers, came to be known, the British commander Robert Pigot set nine of the British warships on fire and sank his transports to block the harbor. Admiral Jean Baptiste Charles Henri Hector, comte d'Estaing, who commanded the French fleet, was anxious for a fight. Unfortunately, the American army wasn't even close to mustering for battle.

The Rhode Island Continentals were still making their way back from White Plains, New York, having been hardened by the long winter in Valley Forge and undergone rigorous training by German soldier of fortune Fredrick von Steuben. They had been battle-tested at Monmouth at the end of June, and by July, Varnum's

Brigade and the 2nd Rhode Island Regiment, accompanied by Glover's Brigade, Jackson's detachment, and the Marquis de Lafayette, were marching back to Rhode Island for the planned assault on Newport.

On July 31, Varnum's Brigade reached Angell's Tavern in Scituate, Rhode Island, where the men encamped and waited for Lafayette's Continentals. The marquis arrived with the troops on August 2, and all immediately departed for Providence. In August, troops from throughout New England marched into nearby Swansea, Massachusetts, and the towns of Bristol, Tiverton, and Providence,[5] the officers generally being welcomed into the finest homes, and the common soldiers encamping in the fields nearby the tavern or meetinghouse. The Rhode Island regiments would spend a week preparing before they were ordered to muster on August 6 and begin the march to Tiverton.

Sullivan's delay in gathering the troops was mostly due to poor transportation. The British had burned nearly every boat in Bristol the previous May, and now vessels were hurriedly being constructed to ferry the troops.

Finally, learning that the British had abandoned positions on the northern end of the island, a contingent of Americans troops under Generals James Varnum and Nathanael Greene began the invasion by rowing troops across from Howland's Ferry at Bristol on the morning of August 9, 1778. The troops landed at the northernmost tip of the island and encamped on a rise called Butt's Hill, which overlooked the long expanse of the narrow island.

At the manned British fortifications, the troops worked against time to shore up the batteries facing the bay and the entrance to the Sakonnet. Lord Richard Howe's fleet finally sailed from Sandy Hook, and showed on the horizon just around noon: "About 12 o'Clock a fleet hove in

At sea off Rhode Island, the British ship *Renown*, left, fires upon the French flagship *Languedoc* that had been left mastless and rudderless following a fierce gale. (*Library of Congress*)

sight to the Southward; 10 Sail of large ships were first discovered. The number increased continually until half past one, when 35 sail, large and small were counted, standing directly for the harbour with a fair wind."[6]

With the arrival of the British fleet, a battle began that pitted the two most powerful navies against one another in Narragansett Bay. As MacKenzie wrote in his diary, "We are now Spectators of two powerful fleets at anchor within a few miles of us, whose operations will probably decide our fate."

In the ensuing days, the French fleet would bombard the British fortifications, and then be drawn out to sea for engagements with British vessels. On August 11 and 12, a fierce gale dispersed the two fleets and wrought severe damage to d'Estaing's fleet. On the 13th, the French flagship *Languedoc*, left rudderless and with its mast shattered, was attacked by the *Renown*, whose guns left sixty French sailors dead, and many more wounded.[7] Another battle at sea three days later left another sixty dead and one hundred wounded aboard the French battleship *Cesar*, after taking a pounding from the British ship *Isis*.

On land, General Sullivan had moved his forces south to establish lines for the siege of Newport on August 15, encountering a line of formidable defenses erected by Sir Robert Pigot and his men from Green End to Tonomy Hill to Coddington Cove.[8] Once established, the troops exchanged cannon fire with the entrenched British forces for nearly a week before word came to Sullivan that d'Estaing intended to take his crippled fleet to Boston for repairs.

When the French left on August 22, Sullivan called a council of his officers. Outraged by the departure, the officers penned a sharply worded, formal protest to the French admiral that nearly destroyed the alliance between the two nations before it had truly begun to take hold. There were further problems as well. Troops from neighboring colonies were deserting in droves, leaving the remaining ranks of the army, according to Lafayette's aide, a "laughable spectacle. . . . All the tailors and apothecaries must have been called out."[9]

According to a report sent to Washington by General Nathanael Greene the next day, the forces under Sullivan's command had shrunk to 8,174 men from the roughly 15,000 who had mustered for the siege just weeks before. Still, when Sullivan sent out general orders to the troops on August 24, he expressed the hope that the remaining American troops would prove able to take by their own means, that which "our allies refuse to assist in obtaining."[10] When word came of the arrival of British reinforcements, Sullivan changed course and decided to lift the siege of Newport and evacuate the island.

In the midst of the drama in Newport, the 1st Rhode Island Regiment had joined the forces in Tiverton. Their mettle was surely tested during the gale, as they hunkered down in the soggy fields above the Sakonnet River, waiting for the command to move into position. As the historian Samuel G. Arnold would note, "In less than six months from the organization of the black regiment it was brought into action by Colonel Greene, and settled conclusively this disputed question of the capacity of colored troops, well drilled and well officered, to make brave and reliable soldiers."[11]

With the change in Sullivan's tactics, the Rhode Island regiments were called upon to play a crucial role in the safe evacuation of Aquidneck Island. The pullback of American forces began the evening of August 24. For the next few days artillery and supplies were gradually withdrawn from the siege lines Sullivan had established to the northernmost part of the island, and the initial encampment at Butt's Hill. On August 28, the forces had formed a line nearly two miles long across the island, extending from a small rise that held an abandoned British redoubt on the western side, to the eastern end of the island, just beyond a crossroad. With the new line established, Sullivan set about to prepare for the defense of the evacuation.

On arrival, Christopher Greene was detached from the 1st Rhode Island Regiment and assigned as brigadier general in command of two regiments, one from Massachusetts, the other from New Hampshire, as well as two militia units from Providence County. Other Rhode Island troops were stationed to Greene's right with Varnum's Brigade and its four Continental regiments.

The 1st Rhode Island Regiment, now under command of Major Samuel Ward, was assigned to guard the abandoned British redoubt that was part of the American line, built on a small rise to the southwest of Butt's Hill. In the distance rose the 220-foot Turkey Hill to the southeast along a dirt road, and the larger Quaker Hill, rising 270 feet to the southeast. Historian Christian McBurney

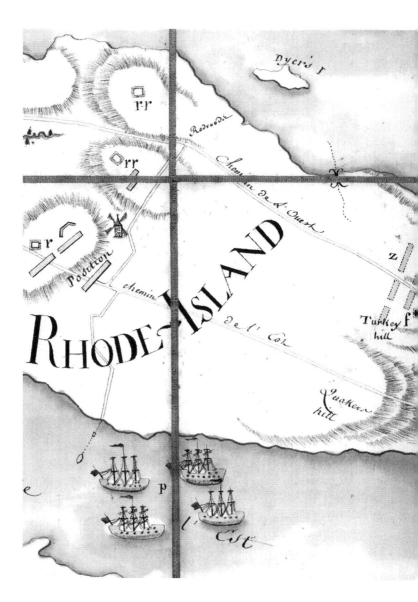

Portion of the "Plan of Rhode Island," by Major Capitaine du Ches-
noy, an aide to Lafayette during the Rhode Island campaign, 1778.
The locations of Quaker Hill and Turkey Hill are indicated, as well as

Butt['s] Hill, near where the 1st Rhode Island was positioned during the battle. (*Library of Congress*)

eloquently renders the scene: "Low rolling meadows interspersed with copses of woods, swamps, and thickets filled the ground in between. Holding this area would be the key to repelling a British attack here."[12]

General Sullivan placed the bulk of his troops at the base of Butt's Hill, some 3,200 men made up of Continental soldiers and state militias from Massachusetts, New Hampshire, and Rhode Island. Sullivan also dispatched two units to delay the enemy's advance. The troops marched out to blockade West Road were under the command of Colonel John Laurens and Major Silas Talbot. The unit sent along the East Road was led by Colonel Henry Beekman Livingston. These troops on the East Road successfully ambushed the British regiment led by Lieutenant Colonel John Campbell, near the Union Meeting House, inflicting heavy casualties.

Lauren and his men were not as fortunate. The battle along West Road began shortly after dawn when Hessian "Chaussers" under command of Captain Frederick von der Malsburg of the von Ditfurth Regiment encountered about one hundred men under command of Major Silas Talbot, entrenched behind the stone walls of the fields intersecting with the West Road and Union Street. The first volley from the Americans sent the Hessians in retreat, where they regrouped and prepared to charge Talbot's position. This time the Hessians drove Talbot's troops back, moving them steadily north for about three miles where Talbot's men took up positions again behind hedges and stone walls below the rise of Turkey Hill.[13]

The Chaussers were relentless, and by 8:30 that morning, the Hessians were atop Quaker Hill and prepared to sweep down through the valley and evict the Americans from the island. For their part, the Rhode Islanders needed to hold their position. The redoubt was the strongest line of defense before the American encampment and their route off the island. More soldiers were placed around the base of the rise where they crouched in the scorched grass, peering through a long valley to the distant hills. On the morning of August 29, the 1st Rhode Island Regiment proved their worth, remaining stalwart in the field, even in the heat of battle.

As the Hessian regiments entered the valley, Generals Greene and Varnum ordered the 2nd Rhode Island regiment and another regiment forward to reinforce the troops protecting the redoubt.

The actions of the Rhode Island regiments received praise from General Sullivan in his letter to Governor William Greene, in which he described a pivotal point in the conflict: "The enemy then advanced to turn our right under fire of their ships, and endeavored to carry a redoubt a little in front of the right-wing. Major-General Greene, who commanded the right wing, advanced upon them with two or three regiments, and being reinforced, drove them back in great confusion. The enemy repeated the attempt three times and were as often repulsed with great bravery, our officers and soldiers behaving with uncommon fortitude, and not giving up an inch of ground through the whole day."[14] Historian Samuel Greene Arnold would write that the 1st Rhode Island Regiment, "Headed by their major, Samuel Ward, and posted in a grove in the valley, . . . three times drove back the Hessians, who strove in vain to dislodge them."[15]

The commander of the Hessians, Captain Malsburg, wrote an account of the battle in his journal, where he recalled that his troops "now rushed up the hill under heavy fire in order to take the redoubt. Here they experienced a more obstinate resistance than they expected. They found large bodies of troops behind the works and at its sides, chiefly wild looking men in their shirt sleeves, and among them many Negroes."[16]

Major Samuel Ward wrote on August 30 that "Our loss was not very great . . . it has not been ascertained yet; and I can hardly make a tolerable conjecture. Several officers fell, and several are badly wounded. I am so happy as to have only one captain slightly wounded in the hand. I believe a couple of the blacks were killed, and four or five wounded, but none badly."[17]

Ward, who had been encamped in Middletown with the Regiment since mid-August, "frequently exchanging shots with the British," was also duly impressed with the performance of his soldiers: "our Picquets and the light corps engaged their advance, and fought them with bravery."

Much has been made of a missive sent to General Sullivan questioning the behavior of the troops in battle. Samuel Greene Arnold's defense of the regiment provides three depositions which allude to a perhaps hurried call to battle by Major Ward.

Most recently, historian Christian McBurney has speculated that they had abandoned their heavy coats once the battle ensued.[18] Given that they had encamped for days during a soaking rain and then labored in humidity preparing for battle, the soldiers might well have cast aside their hats and torn off their tunics in the heat. But to the British, and more especially to the Continentals, the regiment exposed themselves more openly as men of color, fighting side by side with them.

In the aftermath of the battle of rhode island the regiment was sent to Bradford's Hill, near Bristol, as part of Lafayette's division guarding the coastline from Bristol to Swansea, Massachusetts. Some of the regiment was also stationed at Windmill Hill in Warren, Rhode Island. Soldiers spent their days and nights patrolling the shoreline from the mouth of the Warren River down to Poppasquash Point, and up to Mount Hope, Bristol Ferry, and the Narrows. They were given this duty until winter, when they quartered in warehouses along the wharves in Warren.[19]

The following spring of 1779 brought great changes to the regiment. In April, Samuel Ward was commissioned as lieutenant colonel, and reassigned to the Light Corps under command of Lieutenant William Barton in Tiverton.

By May, the regiment had been sent to North Kingstown under Washington's orders to establish a work area for making fascines—the mats woven from the sturdy salt grasses of the Rhode Island coastline and used for making pathways through the swamps for the troops in the southern campaign. Colonel Greene's request to the deputy quartermaster asks for "the necessary tools for making fascines for one hundred and thirty men to work with." This would seem to indicate that only a little more than half of the men Greene had commanded but a year and a half before remained in service. Washington himself wrote that the force at present was "too small to afford any material reinforcement and being usefully employed where it is at present, I have thought it most advisable for it to remain."[20]

The life of the troops was not an easy one. The journals written by soldiers of the revolution depict a dull, repetitious routine of marching, making camp, cleaning weapons, foraging, picking up camp, and marching again. Food, disease, and the condition of clothing were constant concerns.

The young Joseph Plumb Martin enlisted in his hometown of New Haven, Connecticut, at the first opportunity, once he had come of age in July 1776, but by the summer of the following year, he would write that

> No one who has ever been upon such duty . . . can form any adequate idea of the troubles, fatigue and dangers which they have to encounter. Their whole time is spent in marches, especially night marches, watching, starving, and in cold weather, freezing and sickness. If they get any chance to rest, it must be in the woods or fields, under the side of a fence, in an orchard or in any place but a comfortable one, lying down on the cold and often wet ground.[21]

Private John Howland recalled in a letter of 1830, "The men had no bounty when they enlisted, and were not furnished with any clothes; we found our own clothes, and we had the promise of forty shillings per month."[22]

That promise, as with all governmental promises, was contingent upon the Assembly agreeing how to raise the funds needed. Many recruits tired of the military life and returned home once their term of service had ended.

In August 1777, Colonel Israel Angell, who commanded the 2nd Rhode Island Regiment, wrote to the governor and his council, which clearly, from his words, was not the first time he had sent an urgent request. "Pure necessity urges me to trouble you this once more in behalf of ye Troops under my Command," the young colonel wrote. "Not one half of them can not be termed fit for duty on any immergency." Prior engagements with some men marching and fighting in bare feet had exacerbated the injuries received, and, more to the point:

> In fine, ye Regiment is scandalous in its appearance in ye view of everyone-and because of this incurred from

surrounding regiments from ye inhabitants of Towns
thro which they have lately passed, ye disagreeable and
provoking Epithets of the Ragged Lousey Naked Regiment—Such treatment gentlemen, is discouraging
(and) dispiriting in its tendency: it does effectively
unman ye Man and render them almost useless in ye
army(.) I am sorry to have occasion to continue my complaint in their behalf but as I look upon it, a matter, not
of Empertinence but of Importance I cannot refrain in
justice to them.[23]

The young Martin, whose regiment saw action with
Rhode Islanders at Red Bank and later, Yorktown, would
leave an irrefutably honest eyewitness journal from the
war. He would recall later in life that on enlistment, soldiers were promised

One uniform coat, a woolen and linen waistcoat, four
shirts, four pairs of shoes, four pair of stockings, a pair
of woolen, and a pair of linen overalls, a hat or leather
cap, a stock for the neck, a hunting shirt, a pair of shoe
buckles, and a blanket. Ample clothing, says the reader;
and ample clothing say I. But what did we ever realize
of all this ample store—why perhaps a coat (we generally did get that) and one or two shirts, the same of
shoes and stockings, and indeed the same may be said
of every other article of clothing— a few dribbled out
in a regiment, two or three times in a year, never getting
a whole suit at a time, and all of the poorest quality, and
blankets of thin baize, thin enough to have straws shot
through without discommoding the threads.[24]

Martin would note that those memoirs published before his own that told tales of "being tracked by the blood
of their feet on the frozen ground" were "literally true,"
and that "the thousandth part of their sufferings has not,
nor will ever be told."[25]

In August 1779, the General Assembly addressed the growing number of petitions for "allowances" from wounded soldiers, and the issue of pay still owed, voting that the rolls of enlistments be forwarded to the auditor of accounts. The Assembly also addressed the "distressed situation of this state in supplying troops with articles in camp, at stated prices," so they decided to increase their pay, setting for the first time a fixed salary based upon position in the Rhode Island regiments:

Pay of the Militia Officers and Privates per Month
A Colonel, ... $91.33
A lieutenant colonel, ... $72.00
A major, ... $59.33
A captain, ... $48.33
A lieutenant, ... $42.33
An ensign, ... $34.33
A surgeon, ... $52.00
A surgeon's mate, ... $35.00
A sergeant, ... $27.33
A corporal, ... $26.16
A drummer, ... $26.16
A Fifer, ... $26.16
Each private, ... $25.00[26]

In June 1780, the General Assembly passed an act requiring that the State raise an additional six hundred and ten men. In July, the Assembly passed a resolution requesting that Washington pardon all deserters from the State's Continental battalions, and requesting that General Heath "issue a pardon for all the deserters from Colonel Greene's regiment who may join by a time he may think proper to fix."[27]

Colonel Christopher Greene received a letter in late July from the Marquis de Lafayette, relaying instructions from General William Heath:

> As there are some facines prepared on the shore op-
> posite to Connonicut island (Jamestown), it is expedi-
> ent to have them delivered to the orders of the French
> commanding officer—you will therefore, please to send
> a party of four and twenty men, under the command of
> an intelligent, active officer, who will take four boats,
> for which orders have been to the quarter-master, and
> bring over those facines to Connonicut island, as fast as
> it is in your power. . . . General Heath has already de-
> sired that you will immediately send two hundred and
> fifty men, to the same island—he wishes me to add,
> that as soon as you may collect some militia, you will
> also send them to Connonicut, as fast as you can, till
> they amount to three hundred and fifty men—the
> whole of it will form a corps of six hundred men, com-
> manded by a Continental Lieutenant-Colonel, who will
> take orders from the Viscount de Noailles, A French
> Colonel, commanding on the island of Connonicut.[28]

By September, the colony had enlisted five hundred
more men, but in its desperation to fill these quotas,
Rhode Island required all males above sixteen who had
resided in their towns for at least thirty days to register.
This act resulted in one hundred and sixty boys beneath
the age of eighteen enlisting, with one being but fourteen
years of age. In Greene's regiment, the rolls reflect that
of these new recruits, thirty-five men were listed as being
"negro or mulatto," while twenty-eight enlistees were
Native American.[29]

Still, it was not enough. In October, the Rhode Island
General Assembly passed an act requiring the raising of
an additional two hundred and twenty men who would
be required to enlist for three years service. Slaves, or
freemen who enlisted, were expected to remain in the

regiment until the end of the war. In November, an act was passed for an additional three hundred and eight men. This time, the act excluded the enlistment of black and indigenous people.

On January 1, 1781, the 2nd Rhode Island Regiment was merged into the 1st Rhode Island Regiment, Colonel Christopher Greene commanding. Some of the brigade troops were already in Morristown, New Jersey, and the colonel quickly prepared to march his regiment to the front lines, leaving the remaining recruitment to Lieutenant Colonel Jeremiah Olney, who issued the following order:

> Colonel Greene, intending soon to join his Regiment at Head Quarters, mustering the troops will therefore fall upon Major Flagg at East Greenwich, and myself at Providence, where attendance will be given for that purpose on Monday, Tuesday, Thursday, and Friday, till the whole are mustered. Negroes will not be received, nor any but able-bodied, effective men. Preference should be given as much as possible to those who have served in the Continental Army or in the State Battalions.

Curiously enough, the Marquis François Jean de Chastieu, one of Rochambeau's generals, observed the Rhode Island regiment at a Connecticut ferry crossing and noted: "The majority of these enlisted men are negroes or mulattoes, strong, robust men. Those I saw made a good appearance."[30]

At this time however, with the men marching off to certain battle, a number "deserted on the march to Head-Quarters." Between March 10 and April 7, advertisements in the *Providence Gazette* show that twenty-eight men deserted the regiment. A dozen of these were European immigrants from England, Ireland, France, Germany, and Scotland—likely indentured servants or laborers before they signed up for military duties. Nine others had enlisted from out of state, from as far north as Vermont and New Hampshire. Of the remaining Rhode Islanders who deserted at this time, four of them—John Spencer, Robert Vaughn, Thomas Gardner, and John Corey, all of whom had enlisted in East Greenwich—asserted "that they were principled against bearing arms" and desired to return to their Quaker community. Of the remaining four, two were indigenous soldiers, one a "mustee" and the other a white enlistee from Scituate.[31] Four others, of equally diverse backgrounds deserted after the regiment had reached headquarters.

I have purposely stated the mixed races and diverse origins of these men, as some later historians have used these desertions to single out the Rhode Island regiment, and in particular, the former slaves enlisted, as a trouble-plagued brigade of would-be soldiers—even questioning their courage in battle and their place in history. The problem of desertion was constant throughout the war, with soldiers from every state. Roughly, one-third of the army deserted at one time or another.

To compound the matter, they were often sheltered within communities still hesitant to support the revolution, or at least empathetic to the soldiers' plight. Washington had openly grumbled in a letter to Rhode Island's governor Cooke in June 1777 that "The great countenance & protection shown & given to Deserters, by persons in the different Neighborhoods from whence they came, has made that Vice so prevalent in the Army that unless some very effectual Measures are fallen upon to prevent it, our new Army will scarcely be rais'd, before it will again dwindle & waste away from that cause alone."[32] It was a refrain that would be sung throughout the conflict. Washington imposed stricter punishment in the form of whippings, even death by firing squad, as we have seen, for repeat offenders.

But most who deserted did not do so for lengthy periods of time. Many re-enlisted with their old regiment after a general pardon was issued, while others signed on with regiments in neighboring states. The fluidity of troops throughout New England was remarkable in many respects. Men who enlisted with militia did so for ninety days and spent their service mostly guarding the coastlines or assisting with equipment and supplies for the Continental troops. Those men who enlisted in a regiment or battalion of the Continental Line were committed to service for three years.

Throughout the war, men served in a variety of ways, often beginning at a young age with a local militia, where they mustered, marched, and provided protection for their own communities. Many of these signed on with the Continental regiments as the war progressed and climbed the ladder, so to speak, into a junior officer position. Such was not the case with blacks or indigenous peoples, who were long confined to the local militias. But once they were allowed to join, New England states contributed the largest portion of blacks to the Continental Army. A report of those returning from leave in August 1778 records some 755 black soldiers scattered over fourteen brigades.[33] None of these men would ever climb above the rank of private.

A careful reading of Rhode Island's historical records shows that merely a handful of men of color deserted the regiment after it was integrated with the 2nd Rhode Island Regiment.[34] In addition, research shows that of the fifty-eight slaves of African or indigenous descent who escaped from their masters in the years 1774–1783, twelve appear on the muster rolls of the 1st or 2nd Rhode Island regiments. At least three others appear in regiments in adjoining Massachusetts or Connecticut, who also admitted blacks and indigenous men into the army, following Rhode Island's lead. Cato Brown of East Greenwich served in both Rhode Island and Connecticut regiments. Sambo Brown deserted Nixon's Brigade in 1776 but later appears on the *Record of Connecticut Men in the Military and Naval Service during the Revolutionary War.* A Narragansett named Anthony Jeremiah served in a Massachusetts regiment, where his fellow soldiers dubbed him "Red Jerry."[35]

The great majority of those men of color who enlisted in the Rhode Island regiments would serve five full years. Historian Benjamin Quarles notes in his historic work *The Negro in the American Revolution* that "The New England states, despite their relatively small Negro population, probably furnished more colored soldiers than any other section."[36] As Quarles explains, once enlisted, "Negros were less inclined than white soldiers to walk off without official leave. They were not likely to have a farm that needed protection, nor the kind of home that inspired homesickness. They had less to desert to."[37]

It can also be said that the greater number of white soldiers who were integrated into the 1st Rhode Island Regiment also stayed to serve—men such as Thomas Stafford, a laborer, and William Holston, a cooper, both from the village of West Greenwich, who enlisted in March 1777. Similarly, fifers Thomas Mitchell and Joseph Dexter had both enlisted from Glocester in May 1777. All these men served in the regiment until the end of the war.

As historian Henry Wiencek has observed, "There is no record of a popular outcry against the black presence, no record of fights or interdisciplinary problems caused by racial integration. The common white New England soldier seems to have accepted blacks. The objections to the black presence came not from the rank and file but from the highest levels of policy makers and politicians."[38]

The Continental Army was stationed near Fishkill, New York, while Colonel Christopher Greene was sent with the Rhode Island regiment to a location some ten miles distant, at Pines Bridge on the Croton River. They encamped at the so-called "Rhode Island Village," while Greene took up residence in a nearby farmhouse belonging to the Davenport family. Major Ebenezer Flagg Jr. of Newport joined him in mid-April.

Colonel Greene would write in upbeat spirits to Colonel Samuel Ward—a leader in the Battle of Rhode Island—on April 16: "I often very agreeably reflect upon the toils and dangers we have passed through together during the course of this horrid war and nothing could have been more agreeable than to have had your company in command to its close—But this could not be . . . we must therefore for the present be separated. I was overjoyed at the Major's arrival and yesterday went with him to the lines at Pines Bridge where I left him in command. Shall join myself in a very few days." He also, however, alluded to the shortage of men, both from disease and the recent desertions: "We have at present only about two hundred men including officers to guard twenty miles but expect as soon as the men get out of the small pox to have our force augmented to three or four hundred."[39]

Their movements had not gone unnoticed, however, and in the pre-dawn hours of May 14, 1781, a reported two hundred and sixty light horse infantry made up of

Loyalists under the command of Colonel James De-
Lancey forded the river and laid a surprise attack on the
encampment. Early historian William Cooper Nell, in his
book *The Colored Patriots of the American Revolution,* would
write of the bravery of the black men in the 1st Rhode
Island Regiment: "Among the traits which distinguish
the black regiment was devotion to their officers . . .
Colonel Greene, the commander of the Regiment was
cut down and mortally wounded but the sabers of the
enemy only reached him through the bodies of his faithful guard of blacks, who hovered over him to protect him,
and every one of whom was killed."[40]

Colonel Henry Lee offered a different account of
those events once the infantry was heard approaching:
"Greene and Major Flagg immediately prepared themselves for defence, but they were too late, so expeditious
was the progress of the enemy. Flagg discharged his pis-
tols and instantly afterwards fell mortally wounded, when
the ruffians . . . burst open the door of Greene's apart-
ment. Here the gallant veteran singly received them with
his drawn sword."[41]

The colonel does not mention guards of black soldiers
protecting Greene, or taking the thrust of sabers for their
commander, but then, Lee looked with disapproval on
General Washington's orders allowing slaves to enlist. He
was one of the "Southern generals" who persuaded
Washington to hold off on the proposition for so long.
Like his commander-in-chief, Lee was from Virginia and
an impressive horseman. At the time of the attack on
Greene's encampment, Lee's regiment, a mix of light
horse and cavalry troops, had already captured several
outposts in South Carolina and Georgia.

An eyewitness recollection, however, would seem to
suggest that there were numerous people killed within

the house before the dying commander was dragged outside and thrown over the back of a horse. The grand-
daughter of Richard Davenport, who owned the house
where Greene and Flagg had quartered, would recall:

> Word came to us that they were all cut off and killed at
> headquarters, and we ran through the fields to Daven-
> port's house. The Refugees [Loyalist troops] were at
> that moment retreating through the woods towards
> Pine Bridge, and when we saw their glittering caps and
> arms we stopped and hid till they had passed. We ar-
> rived at the house about sunrise, or a little after, and
> found the floors and walls covered with the blood of the
> dead, wounded, and dying.[42]

Among the former slaves in the Rhode Island regiment killed that morning were Africa Burk, Cato Bannis-
ter, and Simon Whipple. Another, Prince Childs, would
die little more than a week later from his wounds.[43] All of
them had been with the regiment since May 1779. More
black soldiers died that morning than white, not with-
standing the success of the surprise attack on the "Rhode
Island Village," and the killing of the commanding officers. Twenty-two men were taken prisoner—the majority
of them being white soldiers of the regiment, encamped
near the river. A pair of black soldiers captured were the
wounded fifer Ichabod Northup and drummer Prince
Jenckes.

Some local accounts say that Colonel Greene had offered to surrender, but was taken from the house and
"dragged into the woods," where he was drawn and quartered. Some credence to the brutality of the corps can be
found in the journal of military surgeon James Thatcher,
who but two months before had attended to those in his
own regiment from Massachusetts, which had been attacked by DeLancey's light horse infantry in Crompton,

New Jersey. Among the testimonies recorded is that of one soldier who told the doctor that he and others had tried to surrender, but were given no quarter by the dragoons.[44] Another account maintains that the wounded colonel's body "was strapped on a horse and started for the British lines. After a mile

Memorial to Colonel Christopher Greene and Major Ebenezer Flagg in Yorktown, New York. (*Author*)

or so the refugees changed their minds, leaving the Rhode Islander's bloody remains by the side of the road."[45]

In his own account of hearing the news of Greene's death, Thatcher recorded that the commander had his guard at the Croton River keep "the greatest vigilance in the night time," but that Greene's habit of "calling off his guards at sunrise, on the idea that the enemy would not presume to cross in the daytime," gave them the element of surprise.[46] This is also given credence in the journal of Jeremiah Greenman, who had but twenty-four hours before been appointed lieutenant of the guard. Greenman wrote that he and the guard were at dawn "alarmed by the appearance of a party of Cavalry supported by Infantry, which proved to be DeLancey's Corps of Refugees / they soon surrounded me and being vastly superior in force—& having no prospect of escape, I thought it most advisable to surrender myself and Guard (as) prisoners of War."[47]

Colonel Christopher Greene's body was found and brought to headquarters the following day. He was buried in a solemn ceremony.

The same morning, Greenman and the other prisoners of the 1st Rhode Island Regiment were "paraded and marched into New York—my men all put into the Sugar House myself paroled to Mrs. Wheatons in Clefts Street a house prepared for the reception of any Officer that migh(t) be made Prisoners 'till they got their parole."[48]

On the death of Colonel Greene, the command of the 1st Regiment of Rhode Island was given to Lieutenant Colonel Jeremiah Olney. In the aftermath of the battle, there were more desertions. Another advertisement in the *Providence Gazette* listed another nine persons who had "deserted."

By June, the regiment was with Washington's troops on the Hudson River, and come September, they had marched with the main Continental Army to the head of the Elk River, where a fleet of transports was ready to ferry the troops to assemble for the siege of Yorktown.

THE COMMANDER OF THE BRITISH FORCES HOLDING YORKTOWN was General Charles Earl Cornwallis. From a distinguished lineage, Cornwallis continued his family's military exploits and became an ensign in the Grenadier Guards at the age of eighteen, and a captain by twenty-one. His reputation grew after a sterling record during the Seven Years' War, and he was promoted to lieutenant colonel of his regiment.

"In America," however, as historian Richard M. Ketchum writes, "his record was spotty, with good performances at Long Island and Fort Lee, and a major failure when Washington's army eluded him and won the battle of Princeton."[49]

He had returned to Britain briefly to care for an ailing wife, and on his return was given a role in the southern campaign, which he eagerly claimed. Cornwallis was determined to stamp out the rebels in North Carolina, while holding onto South Carolina and Georgia. His efforts were costly. As his troops marched through the highlands, many were soon without shoes and became sickly from the heat. Supplies were always short, the men being so far inland from the ships that provisioned them. Skirmishes were all the troops could accomplish, and worse, Carolinians were uncooperative in giving needed information, provisions, or recruits. British supply trains were raided, and dispatch riders ambushed on a regular basis. In March, Cornwallis managed to oust General Nathanael Greene's army from the Guilford Courthouse after a costly day-long battle, during which he had ordered grape shot to be fired into the mass of Americans and British guards engaged in hand-to-hand combat to break up the morass impeding his advance, killing soldiers from both sides.[50]

Greene evacuated Guilford Courthouse and its grounds under cover of darkness, and Cornwallis's troops were too battered to pursue the Americans. By April 1781, he had led his army, which now held roughly half of the original force, into Virginia. Cornwallis's troops engaged Lafayette's Continentals in a game of cat and mouse around the colony that spring, destroying property, including one of Thomas Jefferson's farms, and searching for a proper place in which to lure the Americans and their allies into a pitched battle. Weary of the haranguing letters from Cornwallis on the issue, and the unpredictable movements of his troops, General Henry Clinton finally ordered the general to select a location on which to construct a fortification.

Cornwallis preferred Portsmouth, and then was persuaded to look at Old Point Comfort, a point of land at the mouth of Hampton Roads, a natural harbor fed by the Elizabeth, Nansemond, and James rivers along with smaller tributaries that opened onto Chesapeake Bay. By the end of July, he had reluctantly chosen the city of York, perhaps because it was the choice of Clinton and others, who felt the small hillside town on a high, stone-covered bluff above the York River would provide adequate protection for Hampton Roads. Less than a mile across the river lay Gloucester Point, and its proximity to the Chesapeake Bay, he would discover, left it vulnerable to naval attack.

Cornwallis believed he had well fortified the town, using many of those black men who had sought asylum as laborers to build a set of three redoubts on a slight, pine-covered rise about twelve hundred yards to the southwest, and a star-shaped redoubt to the northeast along the river. Before these redoubts lay abates, a blockade of roots, broken branches, and limbs whose lengths had been sharpened like spikes to deter any advance. But by the end of September, with Admiral de Grasse's French fleet having arrived at his back door, and reports that the Americans were marching from Williamsburg, he abandoned the redoubts on the rise and concentrated on improving the works nearer to the city. Even with the impending battle, Cornwallis wrote confidently to Clinton that "I have ventured these last two days to look at General Washington's whole force in the position outside my works, & I have the pleasure to assure Your Excellency that there was but one wish throughout the whole Army, which was, that the Enemy advance."[51]

During the first week of October, the Americans and their allies transported cannons from the James River, south of the peninsula on which Yorktown lay, to allied emplacements. Other soldiers were employed in digging trenches and improving the abandoned redoubt in the Pigeon Quarter. As these were being improved, sappers dug trenches, zigzagging their way toward the British lines. By the end of the first week of October, the Continental Army had reached within six hundred yards of the enemy lines, having completed a four-thousand-foot-long trench that extended from the river on the southeast side of town to a large ravine. By October 9, the allied emplacements were complete and the assault intensified. Within a few days, the allies had begun to feel assured of their superiority. As Robert Middlekauf explains, "The French gunners, more practiced than the Americans, claimed to be able to put six consecutive rounds in the embrasures of the enemy batteries. The Americans lacked this fine touch but they too fired with an accuracy that distressed the enemy."[52]

Each night the allies pounded the British works, sending those remaining civilians scattering to crudely constructed shelters along the river, while the British soldiers could do little more than burrow into the trenches and hunker down in redoubts. Cornwallis and his advisors huddled in an underground cave. The most vulnerable inhabitants, however, were expelled from the town and left to fend for themselves as the siege continued. These individuals, who had sought refuge with the British, were slaves, many of whom had built the works that were now being obliterated.

Unknown to the black patriots among the allies was that Yorktown had been overwhelmed by slaves seeking asylum. The population had swelled to the extent that British rations were severely depleted by the time the siege began. Smallpox had also begun to spread among them, and as the siege ensued, the Continental soldiers were met by a steady trickle of terrified ex-slaves who

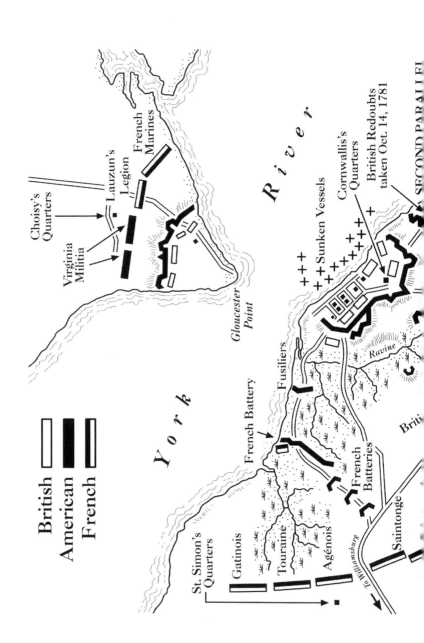

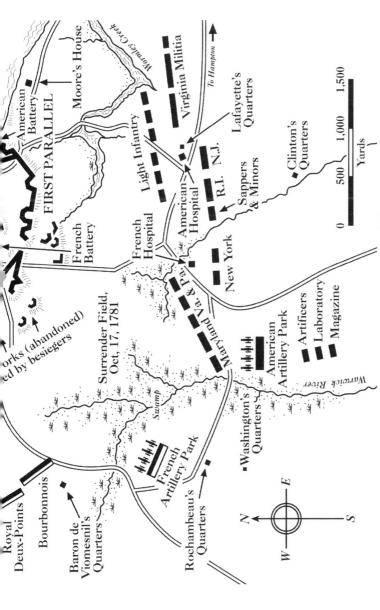

The siege of Yorktown, September–October 1781.

Watercolor of American soldiers at Yorktown, including a private of the 1st Rhode Island Regiment in full uniform by Jean Baptiste Antoine de Verger. *(Anne S.K. Brown Military Collection, Brown University Library)*

had been expelled from the fort.[53] Private Joseph Plumb Martin of Massachusetts would recall that "We saw in the woods . . . Negroes which Lord Cornwallis (after he had inveighed them from their proprietors), in love and pity to them, had turned adrift, with no other recompense for their confidence in his humanity but the smallpox for their bounty and starvation and death for their wages. They might be seen scattered about in every direction, dead and dying, with pieces of ears of burnt Indian corn in their hands and mouths, even of those that were dead."[54]

The British would prove adept at quickly repairing the damage done to the redoubts through the nine days of almost constant bombardment, and answered back with formidable fire from a hundred pieces of cannon. The continual exchange soon rendered an allied assault imperative.

On the evening of October 14, Washington assigned the Rhode Island regiment, which had been placed under the general command of General Lafayette and Colonel Alexander Hamilton, to mount an attack on one of the two remaining British redoubts, while French troops under Baron Vionesnil would attack the other. Lieutenant Colonel Jeremiah Olney, with part of his Rhode Island battalion, were embedded with the 1st and 2nd New Jersey Regiments, under Colonel Elias Dayton and Benjamin Lincoln's 1st and 2nd New York Regiments. A detachment of the Rhode Island Regiment, under Captain Stephen Olney, another member of the prestigious Rhode Island family, was chosen to lead the storming column.

The detachment was determined to storm the redoubt with fixed bayonets, and marched in silence to within two hundred yards of the fort. The column halted and waited while the infantry hacked away abates with axes. Eight men were chosen to lead the charge with swords drawn. As the cries of the Americans reached the British lines, the tories answered the charge with a volley from their muskets. As Captain Olney climbed the hill and forced his way through the palisades, he was wounded by a gunshot in the arm, and by the thrust of the enemy's bayonets in his thigh and abdomen. By then, however, his soldiers had taken the redoubt, the column having entered the fort in the breach of Olney's charge, and the captain regrouped his troops before being carried from the field.[55]

The French faced greater resistance in taking their redoubt, and once it was taken, the British held out two more days, exchanging fire until their ammunition was exhausted. A last-ditch effort by Cornwallis to evacuate troops to Gloucester Point, and rally for an attack on Brigadier Choisy at daybreak to ensure their safe retreat, was thwarted by a storm that rose unexpectedly as the second wave of evacuees shoved off and rowed toward the Point across the river. The general rescinded the order to evacuate and ordered those at Gloucester to return to Yorktown. His demoralized soldiers were rowed back to the besieged city at daybreak, in sight of and under fire from the French and American artillery.

At the sound of reveille, General Cornwallis observed the progress of the allies and inspected his ruined works. When he retired to his headquarters, he ordered a flag of truce and white standard be sent to the enemy lines. He would write to Clinton that "it would have been wanton and inhuman to the last degree to sacrifice the lives of this body of gallant soldiers, who have behaved with such fidelity and courage, by exposing them to an assault, which from the numbers and precautions of the enemy could not fail to succeed. I therefore proposed to capitulate."[56]

Negotiations continued until October 19, when the document of surrender was signed. At 2:00 o'clock the British troops marched out from the ruined fort past "a mile-long gauntlet of French soldiers and marines on the southwest side of the road, and the American rebels on the northeast."[57] Protocol required the defeated general to lead his troops to the field where they would then surrender their arms, but Cornwallis feigned illness and sent Lieutenant General Charles O'Hara in his stead.

The procession lasted for the remainder of the day, with six thousand British regulars and Hessians taken prisoner. Cornwallis and O'Hara were paroled on condition of their remaining apart from the conflict until an appropriate prisoner exchange could be arranged. O'Hara would write the day after the humiliating surrender that "America is irretrievably lost."[58]

WHILE THE 1ST RHODE ISLAND REGIMENT WITH ITS ATTACK on the redoubt had struck the first real blow in the decisive battle of the war, such glory was to be brief for many of the survivors of Yorktown.

After the victory, the Rhode Island Regiment, "now thinned by the casualties of war and the diseases of the camp," was sent with other troops to the transports massing on the Chesapeake. The regiment then undertook "a tedious passage of twenty-one days . . . to the Elk River, whence by easy marches they reached Philadelphia. The small-pox had broken out on the passage, and a virulent fever, unknown and uncontrollable in its character, added to the horrors of the journey."[59]

From November 1781 through March 1782, at least forty-five of these survivors of the Croton River and Yorktown battles would succumb to disease,[60] including Prince

Angell, who died only a few weeks after being promoted to drummer. He and the others who died in the army hospital were buried in what was then the potter's field for Philadelphia.[61] When the long winter was through, the Rhode Island Regiment was seriously depleted, and the call came out once again from the General Assembly for the officers to recruit more men.

In response, Colonel Jeremiah Olney issued the following commentary within his orders: "It has been found from long and fatal experience that Indians, negroes, and mulattoes do not (and from a want of total Perseverance and Fortitude to bear the various Fatigues incident to an army cannot) answer the public service. They will not therefore, on any account be received."[62]

It is interesting to note what at first glance seems Olney's prejudice against enlisting more black and indigenous soldiers into the regiment. Some of this may have been occasioned by his complaint that the troops were poorly trained and prepared for battle; certainly the short time period between recruitment and being sent into battle made for some shortcomings. At the battle of Fort Mercer, he was said to have used the flat of his sword on soldiers who fired over the parapet without aiming their muskets. Olney also felt that in their haste to fulfill the quota, the ranks had been filled by, "imposing improper persons on us for soldiers."[63] Such caution may also be seen in the light of the numbers of former slaves who had died from disease in the months prior to his order.

If Olney feared a new influx of black recruits, he seemed to treat those who served with him with more than a modicum of respect. Later that year, Olney would write an impassioned plea on behalf of one of his soldiers to General Washington:

I beg leave to lay before Your Excellency the Case of Fortune Stoddard a Negroe Soldier of my Regmt who is now in the State of Maryland in Civil Custody in the County of Cecil, for killing one James Cuningham, who with some others bred a Riot in the Soldier's Quarters on the 21st Decr/81, . . . it appears from the Sherriffs Letter the Soldier had his Tryall in June last, and was acquitted of murder but found Guilty of man Slauter, and that from the Laws of the State he will be sold to pay the Cost of Prosecution &c. Except Some person appears to Settle the Charges . . . it appears to me very Cruell, the Soldier should be Sold to pay the Charges, as he was in the line of duty defending himselfe and Quarters against the Insults of the Rioters— I Confess myself at a loss to know the Necessary measures to be persued for Recovering the Soldier again into Service.[64]

One officer whose opinion on utilizing slaves, especially those who had absconded to the British, for his own military purposes, was General Nathanael Greene, who in May 1781 instructed General Thomas Sumter after the surrender of Fort Granby: "Such of the negroes as were taken at this Garrison (as are not claimed by good Whiggs & their property proved,) belonging to the Tories or disaffected you will apply to the fulfilling of your contracts with the ten months Troops."[65] General Greene also tried, unsuccessfully, to convince the legislature of South Carolina to edict the raising of its own regiment of slaves during the Southern campaign, and pressed the idea as well in letters to Governor John Martin of Georgia. Such legislation "cannot fail," Greene wrote, "if adopted to fix their liberties upon a secure and certain footing." The governor's response was supportive, but also bluntly honest in anticipation of its passage: "A body of blacks I am sure would answer every purpose intended; but, am afraid it will not go down with the people here, however, it shall not want my exertions to carry it into effect."[66]

Greene's family was among the Quakers of East Greenwich, and though he was "read out" of the Meeting for his involvement with the Kentish Guard, he grew up in a household led by a minister whose staunch dislike of slavery precluded many of his fellow Friends.. The family's forge in Coventry employed one hundred men, free blacks and whites working together. The patriarch built a fourteen-room house at the Coventry forge and assigned his namesake Nathanael to oversee the works in 1770. There, the younger Greene acquired his leadership skills and amassed a library of military history and law books that neared three hundred volumes.[67]

Despite the governor's promise to push the legislation in for debate, he withheld the proposal until the last meeting of the Assembly, where it was soundly rejected.

THE WINTER OF 1782 SAW EXTENSIVE FURLOUGHS IN THE regiment, as engagements had ended and officers and privates headed home to Rhode Island. Most were required to return on April 1. New enlistments were taken for a service of nine months only, as the General Assembly and the nation's Congress struggled to find a way to pay for the war.

By December of that year, the regiment was discharging their "levies": those men conscripted, drafted, or compelled to serve.[68] One hundred and sixty-four men were discharged from duty at this time. Many of them were still waiting to be paid. As Samuel Greene Arnold wrote, "Great discontent in the army with respect to the half pay for life which had been promised, and which it (Congress) was supposed to commute to full pay for five years . . . but a graver question grew out of the poverty of the Treasury, as to how the army was to be paid at all."[69]

On March 1, 1783, the Rhode Island Regiment was reorganized into six companies, and renamed the Rhode Island Battalion. The newly formed battalion was then ordered to march to an encampment near Lake Oneida, where they would join about five hundred troops from New York under command of Colonel Marinus Willett.

General Washington's plan was to attack the British trading post at Oswego on Lake Ontario. The troops were to wait until a hard freeze had taken hold, when Lake Oneida could be crossed by sleigh, saving a great deal of marching time. The troops set out under cover of darkness, led by a local indigenous guide. They spent a long night marching in snowshoes and found at daybreak that they were within sight of the fort itself, but the element of surprise was lost. The attack was called off, and the soldiers returned to their camp. The march reportedly took a toll on many of the regiment. A number suffered frostbite, and some were disabled the remainder of their lives.[70]

This was the last engagement for the Rhode Island Battalion during the Revolutionary War. On June 2, 1783, two hundred and forty-six men were furloughed by Lieutenant Colonel Jeremiah Olney, to take effect on the fifteenth of the month. Only the "three-year men" who had enlisted in from 1780 were retained, and on December 25, the battalion was disbanded in Saratoga, New York.

4

The Aftermath of War

I N THE GLORY OF VICTORY, AS HISTORY WOULD HAVE IT, only a handful of heroes were chosen for public praise and heroic mention in the early histories of the American republic. Far less was made of the common soldier in those days, perhaps because so many had served in the communities across the former colonies, including Rhode Island. Most of those farmer's sons and white laborers who had eagerly enlisted returned home, as did Thomas Mitchell of Gloucester, Rhode Island.

Mitchell had enlisted in May 1777, telling the recruiter that he was twenty, though evidence suggests he may have been as young as fifteen. Likely his fellow soldiers saw him as little more than a boy even then, for he served six years as a fifer, before returning home. He settled in Gloucester, purchasing a one-hundred-acre farm in 1784.

On December 26 of that same year he married Elizabeth Mathewson of Scituate, and they settled on the farm. Mitchell also remained active in the local militia, serving as a lieutenant from 1788–89, a captain from 1790–91, second major from 1792–95, and eventually becoming a major in 1796. This last posting would place him second in command of the 4th Providence County Regiment. He died at the age of seventy-five, and was buried in the family plot adjacent to an ancient apple orchard where his grave can still be seen.[1]

Levi Weatherhead is on the 1777 military census along with his brother Daniel, and cousins John, Joseph, Jeremiah, Nathan, Amazaiah, and Enoch, who is listed as the captain in the first company of militia. Levi married a woman named Joanna and they had their first son, Samuel, on May 3, 1784. He was followed by a girl named Alpha, born on February 27, 1786, another son named Daniel nearly two years later to the day, and a third son named Levi, born on December 29, 1789. A final son named Preston would be born on November 23, 1791. By the 1820 census, Levi is shown living in a household of seven people including a male and female less than ten years of age, presumably grandchildren, and an elder female, perhaps his mother, Lydia, or his mother-in-law. Two males, assumed to be Levi and a son, are listed as agricultural workers. Levi would receive recognition as a private in the Providence County militia and the State Troops with his pension on September 1833 when he was seventy-four years old. He died on December 3, 1842, at eighty-three years of age and is buried in a quiet cemetery in Diamond Hill, Cumberland.

Stafford Scranton enlisted in North Kingstown for nine months in 1781. He served his time and was discharged on December 19, 1782. Life in the military apparently did not suit him, for he returned home and resumed the life of a laborer. His name appears on the ledgers of Daniel Updike. The grandson and namesake of one of the wealthiest of the Narragansett Planters, the great estate, which had in his grandfather's time held eighteen slaves, was now in decline, and no longer supported by slave labor. By the 1790s, Daniel Updike was overseeing the farm at Cocumcsussoc for his aging father Lodowick, as well as his own concerns in Wickford. The Updikes now hired local laborers for seasonal work, carpentry, or even a few days' labor. These men were paid in all manner of goods.

Scranton began work on the Updike farm on April 1, 1796, and was paid in corn, corn meal, and cash. On November 5: "To one bushel of corn deliver'd Negro Jim per his order . . . " Scranton continued as a laborer on the farm for an extensive period, appearing each year in Updike's ledgers from 1796–1801, and almost certainly worked for Updike, as Smith's Castle was sold in 1812. Scranton appears on the 1818–1872 pension records, where a penciled note indicates he died in 1820.[2]

For those former slaves in the aftermath of the war, we find that the debate about the formation of the "Black Regiment," and their role in the war still took place in political circles as well as within the courts. From the beginning of the enlistment of slaves, some owners had fought the state on the issue. When the act was amended, those owners tested the state on individual cases.[3]

A slave named Prince, owned by John Brown and Nicholas Power, enlisted in Colonel Greene's regiment, as Brown and Nicholas's residence was in Rhode Island. The owners contended however that their slave's place of work was in Grafton, Massachusetts, and that was his residence, not Rhode Island. They took their case before the assembly and won the argument. Prince was discharged from the regiment, remanded to his owners, and ordered to give back "the clothes and bounty which the slave had received from the state . . . and the arms and equipment which the slave had."[4]

The basis of the court's ruling would seem to uphold the institution of slaves as property, or goods at their disposal. Said owners being free to move their goods to various properties they owned, including those out of the colony, said goods were therefore part and parcel of that property while there. A later, similar case concerning a slave purported to be from Groton, Connecticut, was referred to that state's jurisdiction.

Those slaves who had enlisted and served their time and received their freedom were now required to petition the government for payment owed for their service. The commanders who had led the former slaves often came to their defense when they were forced to prove their service. Lt. Colonel Jeremiah Olney gave nothing but praise in his disbandment order for "those brave officers and men he has had the honour to command. . . . Their valor and good conduct displayed on every occasion when called upon to face the enemy in the field, and of their prompt obedience to order and discipline through every stage of service."[5]

Lieutenant Colonel Olney wrote several reports for veterans to obtain their pensions from the government, including Guy Watson, who had marched to Oswego and lost several toes to frostbite. He had enlisted in 1779 and had been discharged on June 28, 1783, for inability to serve due to his injuries. He was not approved for a pension until 1786.

Olney also expressed his outrage to the state at the taking of John "Jack" Burrows, a private in the regiment who was kidnapped while on a voyage to New Orleans in 1791, and kept as a slave. Listed on the 1779 roster, Burrows had served throughout the war to obtain his freedom, but his "master" still held claim to him until Burrows won his freedom a second time in court. He led "a long, if difficult life as a free man and claimed a veteran's pension in his old age."[6]

Many of these men were still due wages, and others had fallen into poverty and petitioned the state for assistance. The federal government continued to struggle to gain revenue from the states. Rhode Island, which would be the last state to ratify the Constitution, would play the part of spoiler in this attempt by the Continental Congress to impose an impost, or tax, on foreign imports to the states.

In February 1781, it was agreed to send an Article to the states approving the federal levy of a 5 percent duty on imported goods, naval prizes, and exported goods. It was the belief of Congress that such a tax would go far in removing the young nation's debt, allow for the payment owed to our European allies, and the pensions of the soldiers who fought in the revolution.

The merchants, who had clamored for revolution through newspapers like the *Providence Gazette*, and incited mob gatherings and incidents like the burning of the *Gaspee*, now declared war upon the tax proposed by the new republic, despite the state's former commander James Mitchell Varnum's status as representative to Congress, being a major proponent of the measure.

While the merchants influenced most members of the assembly, there were others in the state government who stood steadfast in their opposition to any federal imposition on the states, as a violation of those state's rights. In October 1781, Governor William Greene wrote to the new Superintendent of Finance, Robert Morris, that the state had already given its share of cost during the revolution, and proceeded to lay out a general account, telling Morris that he would "easily perceive that this state hath not only fully answered the expectations of Congress, but greatly exceeded their own abilities." Greene wrote that the legislature was understandably cautious, as "at present we are unable to determine upon the utility of that measure, as the revenue arising therefrom, within this little state would not be worth collecting." Greene promised to "wait until our sister states have adopted the same."[7]

This, of course, only delayed debate upon the issue, setting up a series of attacks back and forth from Varnum, whose epistles in the *Providence Gazette* were signed as "Citizen," and rebuttals by the populist mouthpiece of the merchants, attorney David Howell, whose scathing rebukes of the arguments for a federal tax were often signed "A Farmer." Moreover, those merchants in Rhode Island had framed an alternative plan to any proposed tax: the sale of newly acquired western lands. In his work *Rhode Island and the Union*, historian Irwin Polishook notes that "Rhode Islanders had the dream that an enormous revenue might arise from the sale of western lands, perhaps enough to liquidate the costs of the war, as well as provide bonuses, in land grants, to those who had performed military service."[8]

In January 1782, Washington himself wrote to Rhode Island governor William Greene concerning the issue, imploring him to remember the struggles of the past as they looked toward the future: "Your Excellency cannot but remember the ferment into which the whole Army was thrown, twelve Months ago for want of pay and a regular supply of Clothing and provisions, and with how much

difficulty they were brought into temper, by a partial supply of the first, and the promise of more regular supplies
of all in the future." Washington spelled out what was expected in a respectful, but terse tone with the governor:
"There is one plain answer . . . that if the War is carried
on, a certain expence must be incurred, and that such expence must be drawn from the people, either by a par-
tial-cruel, and I must say, illegal seizure of that property
which lays most convenient to the Army, or, by a regular
and equitable Tax in Money or specific Articles."[9]

While the debate continued, and, while waiting for
those states who had still to "furnish the Congress with
substantial security," Congress authorized the Paymaster
General to settle all accounts, and issue certificates for
half-pay to waiting pensioners. These certificates in turn,
became the cause of controversy when speculators, including merchant brothers Nicholas and John Brown of
Providence, took advantage of desperate veterans by is-
suing loans on Continental certificates with exorbitant interest, or buying the certificate outright at a fraction of its
face value.[10] One oft-repeated story is that as John Brown
rode through Providence in a shiny new carriage, one of
these pensioners called out to him "soldiers' blood makes
good varnish," and that the merchant never took the carriage out again.

In June 1784, a committee was enjoined by the Rhode
Island General Assembly, and that September presented
"An Act for the support of the paupers, who heretofore
were slaves, and enlisted into the Continental Battalions." The Assembly acknowledged that "Many of the
said soldiers have become sick and otherwise unable to
maintain themselves," but their ultimate solution was to
place the care for these veterans in the hands of the town
from which they enlisted, declaring, "It shall be the duty

of the town council of the town where such Indian, negro, or mulatto, who was heretofore a slave, and enlisted in the Continental battalions as aforesaid; . . . to direct the overseers of the poor of such town to take care and provide for such."[11]

With the remembrance of the battle cries for freedom still ringing in citizens' ears, free blacks and abolitionists began to use the rhetoric of the Declaration of Independence to advance the fight for those liberties sought with their freedom. But these efforts were met with fierce opposition, and a stubborn obstinacy against those using the rhetoric of the revolution to end the trade. As historian Ira Berlin noted in his thoughtful book-length essay *The Long Emancipation*, "The confrontation of idealism and materialism became entangled as slaveholders drew their defense from the very ideology that stoked opposition to slavery. Revolutionary notions of liberty and equality adopted in state constitutions . . . emphasized the right to acquire, hold, and protect property as an essential attribute of liberty."[12]

In fact, the Constitution ratified in 1789 gave slaveholders a disproportionate representation in the House of Representatives and Electoral College, allowing the importation of slaves into southern states for another two decades, and the Fugitive Slave Act of 1793 protected those slaveholders whose runaways sought freedom in the north. For free men of color, such notions of liberty, tied to the holding of property, proved prohibitive to reach within the confines of the poverty and uncertainty that were a constant in their lives.

The advent of the Fugitive Slave Act allowed local magistrates to issue warrants for the removal of any black person accused of being a fugitive, seemingly on the word alone, of the accuser. It also effectively opened the door

"Kidnapping," an 1822 antislavery drawing showing a woman and child being forcibly removed from their residence in New York. (*New York Public Library*)

for the lucrative trade in kidnapping that became rampant. As Berlin notes: "Kidnappers in the free states and slave traders in the slave states conspired to spirit away hundreds, perhaps thousands of black men and women. Since they cared little about the age, sex, or status of their victims, they swept up men and women who had long enjoyed freedom, as well as those who had but recently gained their liberty."[13] The practice continued unabated until states began enacting "liberty laws" that protected free blacks. Rhode Island, however, did not pass such an act until 1848, long after many of the veterans who had fought for liberty were gone.

The fact of the matter was that those evocations of equality and liberty called for in the famous document did not become part and parcel of the state or national constitutions in the years that followed the revolution. In the aftermath of war, those former slaves and soldiers could not vote in an election if they did not own property. Most former slaves, with a few exceptions, were too poor to own land or a house. They could not ask for the same wages as their white coworkers and could no longer serve in a militia. Their service may have freed them from the shackles of slavery, but they were often in a no-man's land so far as work, equal rights, and status were concerned.

Rhode Island also kept its hand in the slave trade the longest of any of the northern states. While the General Assembly's act in 1774 halted all importations but from the West Indies, which stemmed the flow of slaves considerably, the trade continued amidst the efforts of Rhode Island merchants to fend off the imposition of a national union. Slavers also found ways to circumvent those legislative acts of gradual emancipation, and a 1787 law forbid Rhode Islanders from transporting slaves to international ports. Yet Rhode Island slavers routinely sailed to the Guinea Coast, and sometimes to Mozambique and Zanzibar, where slavers obtained their human cargo and delivered slaves to the Caribbean as well as South America and the United States.[14]

Under the Union, federal law imposed even greater restrictions. The Federal Slave Trade Act of 1808 was intended to end the importation of slaves once and for all, but enforcement proved to be inadequate, and loopholes in the law allowed slavers like captain James DeWolf to circumvent the law.

DeWolf was a native of Bristol, Rhode Island. By the time he was born in 1764, the family was well established in the slave trade. His father had at a young age become the protégé of Simeon Potter, a notorious privateer and slaver. DeWolf expanded the family trade from Bristol, and for years successfully circumnavigated efforts to impound his vessels, fine the captains, or even imprison him. He invested in estates on Cuba, where he held slaves. His wealth and political influence increased, and his fleet of ships became the vessels in which thousands of Africans were delivered into slavery.[15] For many years the histories told us that the last slave ship left Rhode Island in 1807, but research by historian Cynthia Mestad Johnson has shown that James DeWolf was still active in the trade as late as 1824, while serving as a senator for Rhode Island in Washington.

FOR MANY FORMER SLAVES AND INDENTURED SERVANTS, THE life of freedom after the war was also a life of extreme hardship. Some lived independently, existing hand-to-mouth to feed themselves and their families. Others returned to the farms and villages where they had served as slaves or servants. Life as a wage laborer, however, was a precarious existence. Many were hired only at planting and harvesting periods, leaving them to find odd jobs or other menial labor to supplement the wages they earned from their former owners.[16]

In Pawtuxet, Rhode Island, the manumitted slaves of Brigadier General Elisha H. Rhodes began a black settlement around a long cranberry bog off the Post Road just north of the village. This community, as it began to grow, was called "New Guinea" by the locals. Most of those who lived in the makeshift houses along the banks of the bog still worked for families and farms in neighboring Norwood and Pawtuxet. One of the inhabitants was John Lippitt, the son of a servant to an officer in the Revolutionary War, a fact it was said, that he was proud to claim.

Those who had been domestic servants and returned to live with their masters saw little change from the routine they had performed as slaves except for a small paycheck and a day off a week, usually Sunday, when they were required to attend church with the family.

A typical example of the Narragansett Planters' households at the close of the war can be seen in Lodowick Updike's plantation at Smith's Castle, which shows in the 1782 census one "Indian," one "mulatto," and four black servants living in his household of eighteen persons. Among those slaves who enlisted to earn their freedom were Moses and Caesar Updike, then the property of Lodowick Updike. They enlisted together in May 1778. Records show that Updike was paid £92 for Moses, and the maximum £102 for Caesar. Both are listed on the May 1779 muster roll of the 1st Rhode Island Regiment under command of Colonel Christopher Greene.

While records for Moses are incomplete, we know that Caesar served for five years, earning an "Honorary Badge of Distinction," an award given to soldiers who had "served at least three years with bravery." Caesar Updike was furloughed from the Continental Army on June 15, 1783. Like many veterans, he returned to his home state and lived quietly. In the spring of 1795 he returned to Smith's Castle, working as a wage laborer for the Updike family. He was paid in corn, shoes, and sometimes currency.[17] He is listed in the Rhode Island census of 1800 as living in East Greenwich. Like many other veterans, he applied for a pension that was long in coming, not received until April 11, 1818. He died in Kent County on December 13, 1819.

The Daughters of the American Revolution publication of *Forgotten Patriots* also lists a James Updike from North Kingstown. This may have been the James Updike who was once a slave of Lodowick Updike and set free due to the 1784 emancipation act. His record does not show him serving the required time to gain freedom, though he is listed as a "free colored person" and a resident of North Kingstown in the 1790 census, and received his pension in 1831.[18]

Other veterans of the 1st Rhode Island Regiment also worked as laborers on Updike's farm. As well as the aforementioned Stafford Scranton, Joseph Hall is recorded as working two to four days each week during the growing season of 1797. Hall did hoeing, weeding, digging potatoes, and other assorted tasks. He was paid mostly in corn and cash, but received a bushel of apples, a pair of shoes, and "five and a half pounds of fresh pork" in payment, as well.[19]

Some former slaves tried to improve their lot by moving from town to town in search of better wages. A number of them found success, but many were "warned out" from towns in the wake of the passage of the "Act for the support of paupers" in 1784, as the local economy lay in turmoil.

At times, whole families were warned out of Providence, as in the case of Comfort Eddy and his family. Eddy had come to Providence from Massachusetts and was a laborer for a Mr. Sanders, and then for Jacob Whitman. He worked with several blacksmiths and then went to sea for six years before returning to Norton, Massachusetts. He enlisted with a volunteer company under Captain White and served at Bunker Hill.

Eddy then settled in North Providence, enlisted in the regiment from Smithfield, Rhode Island, and served his three years of duty. He returned to North Providence after the war and bought a house and property from Samuel Tucker. Three years later, under unknown circumstances, he removed to Providence once more and "built a small house on the burying place land." By then he had a wife and six children, three of whom were born in Providence, two in North Providence, and one in Douglas, Massachusetts.

On April 9, 1787, the town council rejected the family as inhabitants of the town and warned them to return to

Smithfield, judged to be their legal place of residence.[20] Nonetheless, by the time of his death in February 1819, his obituary reads that Eddy was "in this town, aged about 75 years; was wounded at Yorktown and has since been a pensioner."[21]

Over this period, dependents, widows, and children of Revolutionary War veterans were also "warned out," as was the case with Nan Hull and Sally Saltonstall. In her "examination" before the Providence town council on October 8, 1785, Nancy Hull testified that she "came to Providence with Briton Saltonstall about New Years 1783 but was never married to him. She then had a child by him, three year old Sally Saltonstall."

The child's father, Britton, had enlisted in the 1st Rhode Island Regiment in March 1778, and served for five full years. Saltonstall was discharged on June 28, 1783, "with a pention," and was among those "invalids" who had received a coat in November 1783 for their infirmities. The veteran also appears on the "list of Invalids" compiled in 1785, which described his "loss of all the toes on the right foot and one joint from each of the toes on the left foot." Like many others, he had suffered frostbite during the ill-fated Oswego expedition. Records show that Saltonstall continued to live in the Providence area, though he was apparently unable to support his former partner and daughter. Instead, Nancy Hull and her child were removed to New York, which was "adjudged to be their last lawful place of residence."[22] Saltonstall would not receive a large payment until March 1789, and he received another lesser payment a year before his death in 1816.

Men who returned and found unfavorable circumstances might fade from the community's historical memory altogether. Such were the unfortunate cases of Nathan

Jones and Prime Brown. As a young man of sixteen, Brown had enlisted for service in 1775 from the agricultural community of Johnston, Rhode Island, and was a slave of Gideon Brown.[23] He is listed on the 1777 military census, and in later musters he is listed as Prime or Primus.[24] He served until the 1st Rhode Island Regiment was disbanded in December 1783.

"Nathan" Jones, as he is registered in the regiment book, also enlisted in Johnston and left $100 in silver with his former owner, Benjamin Waterman, for the care of his children, should he fail to return. Jones died while with the army on January 9, 1782. He left a widow, Eunice Phenix, and two children.

After the war, Prime Brown returned to Providence and took in the widow Jones and at least one of his children. At some point in the next few years, while living with Brown, Eunice Phenix died. Brown's name does not appear in any legal documents or in the court records of Providence from the time of his discharge from the army.

In April 1787, however, the Town Council met to discuss the fate of Margaret Abbee, alias Margaret Harris, who was the common law sister-in-law of Nathan Jones. Margaret was born in North Providence and had married Tobias Harris at the age of eighteen. Tobias was the servant of Christopher Harris of Providence, and Margaret moved to the city to live with her husband. By 1787, however, Margaret and her two children found themselves destitute and at the mercy of the town.

After the council heard her case, the town clerk was ordered to write to the town council of Johnston, which read in part: "That Nathaniel Jones a Free Negroe Man who heretofore lived in the Town of Johnston and enlisted in the Army of the United States and there died has left Two Children One of them called Katherine aged about Six Years, and the other Nabby, aged about Seven Years, born to him by Eunice Phenix, with whom he lived and is also died. Is that the children are Orphans destitute and likely to be chargeable to the Town."[25]

The clerk informed the Johnston town council of the "representation" that Jones had left "one Hundred dollars Silver Money" for the child born in Johnston and requested that "Your interposition and Assistance That the Money may be appropriated to the Support of the Child, or children by calling upon Mr. Waterman therefore—It is said that a Place is procured for the One which was born in this Town But the other is chargeable to the inhabitants here and being a legal inhabitant of Johnston must be first there to be provided for." Providence warned the family out, ordering the warrant that would "remove them immediately."[26]

Margaret Harris told the council of another likely "chargeable" resident of the town, Kate, the surviving seven-year-old daughter of her deceased sister Eunice, who had left the child with Prime Brown, with whom Jones had served in the Rhode Island Regiment. The town investigated and, as the child named Kate Jones was determined not to be Brown's daughter, ordered the seven-year-old removed to the town of Johnston, where she had been born.[27]

The life of Prime Brown thereafter seems to have taken a downward spiral, and he was apparently destitute and possibly homeless in November 1819, when he was "found dead in a lot near the Friends Boarding School." Brown, who is listed as "colored," was determined to be "about 70 years of age." He was in fact eighty years old, and his brief obituary makes no mention of his military service. Such a tragic outcome underscores the risk that many took in enlisting for war in exchange for the promise of freedom.

The story of those former slaves who adapted and lived quietly within the mainstream of white society have been well documented by others, such as the cases of Jack Sisson, Winsor Fry, Prince Greene, and Guy Watson. Perhaps the most famous of these, for a time, was Sisson, whose actions in one adventure early in the war were to give him fame and enliven the cause for blacks to bear arms.

Jack Sisson was an African American originally from New Shoreham (now Block Island) and he volunteered with Captain Thomas Cole's company, of Newport. He later served two years in Capt. John S. Dexter's company as a "waggoner." But it would be his innate skills as a mariner that would cause him to be part of one of the most daring exploits of the war.

During the occupation of Newport by the British, the commander of the troops occupying the island was General Richard Prescott. Among the loyalists in Newport at the time was a distiller and merchant named Henry John Overing. At some point during the occupation the general and merchant became friends, and the commander was soon spending a great deal of time at Overing's farm.

American spies soon learned of the general's laxness during his visits to Overing, which were often in the evening. He often brought only a guard, and assumed the quiet of the Portsmouth countryside gave his movements a cloak of safety.

So it was that Jack Sisson, then among the 2nd Rhode Island Regiment, became part of a plot to kidnap the British general and exchange him for the American General Lee. On the evening of July 10, 1777, a flotilla of five boats carrying forty troops traversed Narragansett Bay, rowing between Patience and Prudence Islands to avoid the British warships, and made land at the Bristol Ferry.

The capture of British general Richard Prescott, July 10, 1777.

Sisson piloted one of the boats through the bay, and by at least one account accompanied the troops down the road to the Overing farm. Once there, the lone guard was easily overtaken, and the troops entered the home to find the British general cowering in bed behind a locked door. As Benson Lossing's 1851 *Field-Book of the American Revolution* would have it, Sisson, "a powerful negroe," head-butted the bedroom door, and the general was dragged from his room in his nightclothes, pleading for an overcoat. The boats returned to Warwick Neck without incident, and Lee was exchanged for the American's prisoner some months later.

While the role of "the Black man" listed with Barton's raiders would be attributed to at least three others, including Guy Watson, historian Christian McBurney concludes after his own extensive research that "If a man of color did batter down a door at the Overing house, then it probably was Jack Sisson."[28]

By the time Sisson became part of the integrated 1st Rhode Island Regiment in 1781, his fame and reputation had likely preceded him. He would survive the battles and skirmishes of that active and costly year, only to die with more than forty other men during their winter encampment in Philadelphia.

Winsor Fry first appears in the will of his owner Thomas Fry, written in December 1773 as "A colored man named Winsor," bequeathed with other property to his son John. Winsor Fry enlisted in the Continental Army in 1778 to earn his freedom but seems to have given in to the temptation, as many others did, of stealing from army supplies to make a small profit from eager local merchants who sold the goods at greatly marked up prices in their mercantile stores. While stationed in Morristown, New Jersey, Fry was brought up on charges in a military court on May 28, 1780, for breaking into the commissary and "stealing from thence a quantity of beef, candles, and Rum." He was also accused of breaking into a pair of windmills and stealing meal. The soldier pled guilty, but rather than showing the prisoner mercy, the military court took into consideration previous bad behavior and brought down a sentence of death. Washington, however, who had to approve such rulings, refused to do so, writing to the court: "As I never wish to inflict a punishment, especially capital, but for the sake of example . . . you have my consent to pardon him."[29] Winsor Fry was a model soldier thereafter, and returned to East Greenwich after the war where he married a woman named Lucy. They had one son named Solomon, born in 1788, who would become "a much respected colored man" in the community and build a small house in the town where his father was once a slave.[30]

Prince Greene, one of the many servants of Richard Greene, had worked as a laborer on the family farms in Coventry and West Greenwich.[31] Prince had run away from his master in 1776, as shown in the "Desertion Notice" placed by Greene in the *Providence Gazette* in May of that year.[32] Prince is listed in the 1777 military census and was no doubt eager to enlist in this opportunity for freedom. He married Rhoda Eldred of East Greenwich on June 21, 1778, but remained in the regiment, serving four years and six months as a private, and earning a badge of distinction.

Greene was also exceptional in being one of a handful of black soldiers to face court-martial, after an incident on April 10, 1781, in Providence. The town was still under martial law, though young residents often challenged the local militia and Continental troops after a night of carousing. That night in April, a twenty-three-year-old Providence man named Edward Allen, in the company of another man named John Pitcher, approached the barracks and began to throw stones and hurl "illiberal language" at the soldiers inside. At some point, the two kicked open the barracks door where a voice in the darkness warned them to get out before they were fired upon. Particulars of the incident are unclear, but at some point as the men were running from the scene, Prince Greene followed them outside and fired his musket. The ball struck Allen in the back of the head, mortally wounding him.

The incident caused an uproar, especially as a black soldier had fired the fatal shot at a white resident. As the state's Supreme Court was sitting in Providence at the time, Greene was brought to trial just four days later. He was defended most ably by David Howell, a prominent attorney who was friends with Colonel Christopher Greene, and other high-ranking officers of the Continental Army. Prince Greene was found "not guilty of willful murder but manslaughter," and he was accordingly branded with an "M" on his hand, and eventually allowed to rejoin the regiment. The victim's mother, Elizabeth Allen, outraged by what she saw as a lack of justice, commissioned the Hartshorne gravestone carvers of Newport to furnish his stone in Providence's North Burial ground which recounts his "misfortune of being shot by a negro soldier," an act "Most barbarously done."[33]

Though free after the war, Prince Greene also faced years of poverty. He appears on the "List of Invalids resident in the State of Rhode Island" of 1785, describing his injuries as "the loss of all the toes and the feet very tender, by means of severe frost, when on the Oswego expedition."[34] A fiddler, Greene sometimes bargained with merchant William Arnold for violin strings in exchange for "1 evening fidlen."[35] He was a fixture at events in town for many years, as one description of the black neighborhood of the 1820s describes: "On the infrequent holidays the young men amused themselves in the lots, playing ball, shooting at poultry . . . but the highest frolics were the large quilting parties. After the quilt was finished . . . a dance was next in order. The music was supplied by the violin of an old negroe named Prince Greene, one of the servants of General Greene."[36]

Guy Watson was enlisted in South Kingstown. He was the slave of James Watson, whose farm was one of the larger plantations in South County. It seems likely at this early stage of the war that Watson was signed over by his owner in place of a family member drafted for enlistment. Watson would serve for five years, earning distinction at the battles of Red Bank and Ticonderoga. He would reenlist in 1778 and eventually marched with others on the Oswego expedition and suffered severe frostbite, especially to his right foot, which would leave him disabled for the remainder of his life.

Watson would return to South Kingstown and assume a prominent role among the slave community, serving as Chief Marshall, and "governor" of his black community, elected in the famous "Black Elections" of the day. These evolved from traditional African celebrations to a selected day, or several days, where the black population would gather, usually the third or last Saturday in June, and amid much eating and dancing, choose those "rulers" who would oversee the well-being of their community. Local writers often wrote about these occasions with bemusement, as Robert Hazard noted when he described the slaves borrowing of clothes and finery, even the horses as they left their plantation with "heads pomatumed and powdered, cocked hat, mounted on the best Narragansett pacers . . . pranced to the election."[37]

Such elections, though with perhaps less finery, were also held in Warwick, where for at least sixty years the black community of "New Guinea" held annual elections to choose a new governor. The last election was reportedly held in 1837, at the Golden Ball Inn. Alfred Fisher, a lifelong resident of the village and its postmaster in old age during the Civil War, recalled his younger days, when he had attended several of these events, and "well recalled the excitement of the electioneering and the voting, which the elders tried to keep as dignified as possible." For many years in Pawtuxet, John and Thomas Lippitt, the sons of the aforementioned veteran of the Revolutionary War, dominated these elections. Fisher recalled that on Election Day, "Each nomination was made in a flowery speech which sometimes bore a ludicrous similarity to the bombast of the white political orators of those days. When the nominations had been made and been seconded by numerous voices, the crowd separated for the voting, those on the right being for one candidate, those on the left for the other." The elected governor "had no authority but the position carried a lot of prestige and was eagerly sought after," in both communities of Pawtuxet and South County.

In fact, research has shown that these elected governors, like Guy Watson, actually played an important role in relations between local slaves and masters. These men served as intermediaries when conflict occurred between slaves, and even addressed abuse by certain masters. In addition, these former slaves and veterans likely honored these elections as an echo of the promise given when they fought for freedom. The mock-speeches and voting made the celebratory afternoon a day of self-proclamation for the black residents, who fully knew, as historian William D. Piersen explained in his book *Black Yankees*, "Whites seem to have gone along with these black elections because they hoped they could use the resultant black governors as indirect enforcers of social propriety; moreover, since the whites saw the black elections and festivities as humorous, non-threatening imitations of white traditions, they did not perceive the celebrations as a threat to the social order."[38]

The same may be said of the black "militias" after the war, one being the Washington Cavalry formed around 1790 for ceremonial purposes. The black men who rode on the white horses in parades were not armed, but were resplendent in their cockaded hats, buttoned frock coats, and black boots. Surely those veterans took pride in dressing "in uniform," and reminding their community that black soldiers had also fought in the revolution.

Guy Watson lived until 1837, leaving a daughter, Sarah Hazard, at whose house he died. His funeral was attended by local farmer Daniel Stedman, who recorded in his diary that "I and Wm Nichols went to the Funeral of Guy Watson (a man of Color), one of the old pentioners . . . he was buried on J. B. Dockey's place near Kingston."[39] His obituary would credit him for the heroic role in the Barton raid to kidnap General Prescott. While Watson made no mention of this act in his pension application, the legend of his presence there grew as the veteran reached his final years and, by the time of his death, came to be accepted. Such was the revered soldier's esteem, it is likely that many heroic acts were attributed to him.

In a number of early histories we find anecdotes and half-wondering tales of some of these black veterans, such as the life of one of the servants of Colonel Christopher Greene as told by Oliver Payson Fuller: "Col. Greene had a negro servant . . . named Boston Carpenter who was one of the wonders of those times. By diligence and economy he accumulated some property in Coventry, at the foot of the ridge called, after him, 'Boston hill.' He purchased his wife of Job Greene, for 4s. 6d . . . to prevent her becoming chargeable to the estate of Job Greene, in case she should be reduced to poverty."[40] Carpenter was also, Fuller writes, "a famous breaker of horses, an active mechanic and a quick, sharp man." He lived a half mile north of the village of Anthony, and tended Job Greene's gristmill in Centerville for many years.

Others, such as Ichabod Northup, blended into the community as well. Ichabod had been born into slavery sometime after 1745, and was one of ten slaves who worked on John Northup and his father Emmanuel's farms in North Kingstown. He enlisted in the 1st Rhode Island Regiment in 1778 and trained with others at Academy Field in East Greenwich. Camped within the Rhode Island village at Croton River, he was captured and held as prisoner for two and a half years, thus making approximately half of his five years served as a prisoner of war.

He returned to East Greenwich and worked as a laborer, married, and raised a family. Ichabod Northup purchased a house in 1816, a testament to his hard work, as he did not receive his pension until a few years later. He died in 1821, and for another twelve years his family continued to live in the house, which can still be found on Division Street.[41]

Richard "Dick" Rhodes also enlisted "for the duration of the war" at the age of twenty. He is listed as having been born in Guinea, and a laborer in Cranston. He served for five years, earning one badge of distinction, and was furloughed with others on June 15, 1783. Rhodes returned to his community of Cranston. He received a pension of December 31, 1789, and also worked as a laborer until January 1821 when he was "found frozen in the road south of Pawtuxet."[42]

Despite the hardships faced by those veterans of the 1st Rhode Island Regiment, perhaps the most eloquently stated reasons for enlistment were spoken by one Dr. Harris, when as an elderly veteran in 1842 he addressed the Congregational and Presbyterian Anti-Slavery Society at Francestown, New Hampshire. He told the gathering, "Then liberty meant something. Then, liberties, independence, freedom, were in every man's mouth. They were the sounds at which they rallied, and under which they fought and bled. They were the words, which encouraged and cheered them through their hunger, and nakedness, and fatigue, in cold and in heat. The word slavery then filled their hearts with horror. They fought because they would not be slaves. Those whom liberty has cost nothing do not know how to prize it."[43]

OF THE NARRAGANSETT MEN WHO SERVED, AMONG THE youngest was Henry Matthews, who enlisted in 1779 in Newport at the age of sixteen. He served as a private for four years, including in the 5th Company of the Rhode Island Battalion, under Lt. Colonel Jeremiah Olney, earning one badge of distinction. Asa Babcock and John Mumford, both eighteen, enlisted at Westerly and South Kingstown, respectively. Both served with their fellow Narragansett in the 5th Company for three years. Daniel Perry, twenty-two, enlisted at Charlestown in December 1780. Among the oldest to enlist was Narragansett John George, at thirty-nine, who enlisted in Charlestown in 1780. George was one of those captured at Pines Bridge in May 1781, and was not released until September, when he rejoined the regiment. He served for three years, being discharged on December 25, 1783. Ephraim Charles, who enlisted at the age of thirty-seven, served three years as well. The DAR muster lists another seventy indigenous men who served in the 1st Rhode Island Regiment for part or the majority of the war.

In some instances, extended members of a Narragansett family enlisted. Such was the case with the Harry family, who contributed five members to service in the Continental Army. John, Gideon, Silas, Daniel, and Christopher are on the DAR rolls. John enlisted at Charlestown when he was eighteen years of age. He is listed on the 1781 muster roll as enlisted for three years. He served as a drummer in the 1st and 2nd Rhode Island regiments. Gideon may have enlisted at the same time. He is listed as enlisting "from desertion" in March 1781, but by May was listed as a deserter again. It may be that he fled with others from the surprise attack at Croton River to avoid being taken prisoner. Silas, Daniel, and Christopher served out the war and returned home.

The Perry family has a long military history, beginning with Auguontis, who challenged the governor's appointment of the Niantic Sachem Ninigret, over control of the Narragansett. Auguontis's grandson Abraham would join British forces during the Old French and Indian War in 1760, serving with Captain Russell's Rhode Island company, and later served in the Revolutionary War. The family's oral history tells us that Abraham was a Narragansett warrior who was instrumental in leading reservation Indians in the fight on Rhode Island soil. Earning the sobriquet of Commander Perry, because of his age and leadership, he led indigenous troops during patrols and in the important tasks of clearing land and building stone walls and fortifications.

His son Peter Perry also " preferred war to farming" and enlisted in 1777. He survived the war and on his return to Rhode Island he kept his family's lands intact and preserved more than 180 acres more of tribal lands. Peter married Elizabeth Hoxie on June 8, 1794, and continued to live in Charlestown. The 1810 census shows him as the head of a household with five children.

The sons of Margaret Perry and John Anthony would serve as well in the Rhode Island regiments. John Anthony would serve in the 1st and 2nd Rhode Island regiments, enlisting in February 1781, and is on the December 26, 1783, report of the "Three Years Men" facing their end of service, John having served two years, ten months, and nineteen days by that date. Brother Elisha would enlist in the town of Johnston, where he lived at the outbreak of the war.

Among other Narragansett men, Joseph, Joffrey, and Peter Couchop are on the rolls as well. Joseph and Joffrey served in the regiment, while Peter served aboard the sloop *Independence*. Built in Baltimore in 1776, the Continental sloop guarded merchant ships plying the Atlantic to the Caribbean Sea. In 1777, it was engaged as a dispatch ship on a diplomatic mission to France and hosted Commander John Paul Jones of the *Ranger* while the sloop was anchored in Quiberon Bay in February 1778.

With their traditional relationship to Narragansett Bay, many indigenous people joined the ranks of sailors or merchant marines during the war. Narragansetts John Perry and John Nocake served as seamen aboard the *Alfred*, which had an illustrious history.

Built as a merchant ship and christened the *Black Prince*, it was acquired by the Continental Navy in November 1775, renamed, and refitted as a warship; it saw action in the Battle of Nassau and was engaged in the capture of the British schooner *Hawk* and the brig *Bolton*. Nocake also served aboard the sloop *Providence*, which had sailed with the *Alfred* as part of the fleet in the assault on Nassau. Christened the *Katy* in 1775 under command of Captain Abraham Whipple, it cruised the coastal waters to protect merchant ships departing and arriving in Narragansett Bay. It sailed to Bermuda in September 1775 in an effort to intercept a packet ship containing gunpowder. On return, the vessel was renamed and temporary captain John Paul Jones was given command on May 10, 1776.

Under Jones' leadership, the sloop made a number of significant captures. In September alone, after departing the Delaware capes and heading to Nova Scotia, the *Providence* took seven prizes, burned a British fishing schooner, and sank another before returning to Providence in early October. With the British capture of Newport in December, the sloop lay retired until breaching the blockade in February 1777, under command of Lieutenant Jonathan Pitcher. It continued as a successful privateer until July 25, 1779, when it was destroyed by the crew to avoid falling into British hands during the failed Penobscot expedition.

Other Nocake family men on the muster rolls included John and James, who served in the 2nd Rhode Island Regiment, as well as Gideon Nocake, who enlisted at the age of thirty-five for three years of service. Nearly a hundred years later, facing the committee that would eventually illegally detribalize his people, Gideon's grandson spoke proudly of his legacy among the Narragansett people: "My Grandfather in his time, stood second in the council for years and years. He was a member, went to the Revolutionary War, and came back, and lived and died at home."[44]

The indigenous Rhode Island soldiers' contribution to the Revolutionary War was remembered well into the twentieth century through oral history, and occasionally in print. The December 1935 edition of the *Narragansett Dawn* has a remembrance of Mrs. Lucy Miles, whose family included "male members" who had "served as Soldiers in the Colored Regiment in the Revolutionary War."[45]

Princess Redwing, in her address to the ladies of the Woonsocket DAR, told the story of Simeon Simons, a Narragansett who attended Dartmouth College and "received the first degree in 1777. Then he joined the Continental troops and fought for liberty from the tyranny of England. Having an education, he fought side by side with your ancestors and for the same cause, although your gain meant in reality his loss, as far as land and material things went." She told the gathered DAR ladies, "Back in those days the Narragansett did not count his wealth by his lands, but by what these hills, forests, and shores could give him, a livelihood."[46]

Princess Redwing later elaborated to a reporter from the *Woonsocket Call* the story that Simons and others had gathered on the village green in Patchaug, Connecticut, to greet General George Washington. The general had been struck by the clear, blue eyes of the indigenous boy, and chose him on the spot to accompany him. Simons became a life-guardsman for the general through the duration of the war.[47]

While existing records cannot corroborate her family story, the records of the 1st Rhode Island Regiment list Simons as from Norridge, Connecticut, enlisting at Stonington in 1781 at the age of sixteen. He served as a private until being discharged on December 25, 1783.

Of those Narragansett men who served in the Revolutionary War, the record shows that only a handful among them, including Henry Matthews and John George, applied to the federal government for a pension. Matthews received his in 1794, and George appears on the pension list but without a recorded date of his approval. This was not an uncommonly low percentage of those who had served. As John Howland wrote of those surviving veterans in a letter to Benjamin Cowell, Esq., in 1830, "I know of not more than six or seven now living, who have asked to be placed on the list."[48]

Most of the Narragansett, like the Nocakes, simply went home. But as they and others who returned from service found, this was not an easy matter. In February 1785, members of the Narragansett filed a petition from Charlestown, which was read before the General Assembly that month, "regarding lands taken from Indians and given to others while the original owners where away as soldiers in the Continental service."

In this instance, the lands seized and given to others were taken by the tribal council, as in the cases of Joseph

Jeffrey, and "likewise Land that was given by the King & his Council unto Gideon Nocake, they have taken it away and Given it to James Wappy, when the said Nocake was a soldier in the Continental service."[49] The same occurred with land owned by Daniel Perry. The tribal council also took land from the heirs of James Pall. The petitioners also claimed that the council had "sold wood off a number of Indian Land and further they have Taken the Fort Neck which was Granted for the benefit of the King's Hears (Heirs) and converted the Rest of it to there own use." Such action has precedent within the tribe as in an earlier case involving James Niles of Brothertown, when the council took the stand, with which the courts ultimately agreed, that he could not sell land to a white man, and that if owners or heirs who owned the land were away for a great length of time, or no longer put the land to use, such resources should not go to waste and were thus put to use for the welfare of the tribe.[50]

The council had reason for concern; in 1779 the body told state authorities that, "There are many more now among us that are about Leasing out their Lands for a great Number of Years & moving away among other Tribes & Principally those who Possess the best Farms."[51] The fact that only a few months after the petition signed by Noka and Perry, Samuel Niles filed another petition signed by eighty-three members of the tribe for state oversight of their lands seems to suggest that if this was a continuation of policy, a significant number of tribal members now sought to retain some control over their own, individual properties.

Daniel Perry found himself in the same straits after his discharge on December 25, 1783. He too signed the petition and later married a "free black woman" named Ruth. They had a daughter, born in South Kingstown and registered as "black," a year later.[52] Perry is listed on the census in Washington County of 1790 and 1800 as a farmer and a "free colored man." A decade later Perry and his wife had moved to Kent County and were living within a household of seven people, including one child under ten who may have been a grandchild. In 1840, the year of Perry's death, he and his wife are listed in the United States Census as "free colored persons." The couple now lived alone on their small farm, hiring one white man to assist with the work.

With his choice to marry a free black woman and have children with her, Perry would lose his official identity as a Narragansett man. This was, in the words of one Narragansett historian, the beginning of a "paper genocide" of their people. It is a widespread belief within the Native Americans of the region that there were both written and unwritten policies throughout New England to erase indigenous people and their communities. Using terms like "colored" in the public record was a way to assimilate and eradicate tribal communities.

The same would occur within the Nocake family, when nearly sixty years after the close of the war, Joshua Noka, the grandson of the Revolutionary War soldier, would be listed in the 1840 census as a "colored" man, along with his wife and children.

Though they remained Narragansett within their own households, extended families, and within the tribe, the importance of losing such status in the government record would be realized with the state's advances to detribalize the remaining Narragansett, beginning in 1846, and based in great part upon the tribe's "dwindling numbers." By 1879, the General Assembly formally met to "Inquire into the Justice, Expediency, and Practicability of abolishing the tribal relations of the Narragansett Indians, of

Conferring the rights of citizenship upon the members thereof." Despite eloquent protests from tribal members over the next two years of public hearings, the General Assembly voted in 1881 to strip the tribe of its title and property. Their land would be sold with benefits from the sale going only to those who could unequivocally prove that they were of Narragansett origin. Many whose families had been mislabeled as "colored" on census and birth certificates in the decades after the Revolutionary War would now have to fight again for their homeland.

Despite the legal policies that sought to determine who was or was not indigenous, the Narragansett, like other Native Americans within the region, made hard choices to survive economically, while preserving their language, culture, and art, their political consciousness and beliefs, even in the most difficult of circumstances. Detribalization did not prevent the Narragansett from maintaining their traditional government, or from recognizing sachems, the tribal council, medicine men and women, as well as tribal prophets, the war chief, clan mothers, and others of authority within the tribe.[53]

FOR MANY OF THESE COMMON SOLDIERS OF THE REVOLUTION, the true recognition of their service came only with death, as shown in this obituary for Richard Cozzens, which appeared in the *Providence Journal* on December 24, 1829: "COZZENS, Richard, colored, age about 80 years, a native of Africa; brought to America when very young; many years a slave in family of Matthew Cozzens at Newport; was in the Revolution 5 years, as a fifer; served in regiment, commanded by Col. Christopher Greene, and afterward, Col. Jeremiah Olney, lived in Providence since his discharge from the army in June, 1783."[54]

Likewise, the "generally loved and respected" Christmas Hunt, who died at 100 on February 24, 1822, was "born at Bristol, R.I. in 1722, his parents both Africans, he was a soldier of the Revolution and retained the martial spirit for many years carried newspapers in his vicinity, he used (to) anniversary and parade days turn out with the Ancient Artillery of Providence, dressed in his Revolutionary uniform."[55]

Cozzens was likely joined at these gatherings and ceremonies by John Strange, a fellow soldier in the Rhode Island Regiment, and a poor white laborer in Newport in 1777, when he enlisted at Providence "for the duration of the war." Strange died in Swansea in 1827 at the age of seventy, and, his obituary informed readers that he was "a Revolutionary pensioner; was a drummer, he beat the drum at the 50th anniversary of Independence at Providence."[56]

But such laudatory words of remembrance did not guarantee that any other memorial would be given. Many former slaves who became veterans of the Revolutionary War were buried in a pauper's grave, others in unmarked or temporarily marked graves on the farms where they labored. Still others were remembered with tombstones in public burial grounds, though these seem to be few. Among the grave sites registered as belonging to members of the 1st Rhode Island Regiment by the Sons of the American Revolution in 1929, a handful were those of these former slaves.

Caesar Wheaton and Charles Freeman are buried in Providence's North Burial Ground, and while staff could approximate locations, the author could not locate their gravestones, many in the area being worn and illegible after two hundred years or more. Wheaton served for a little less than two years in Captain Elijah Lewis' company of Greene's regiment. Charles Freeman was born in Massachusetts and was listed as a laborer there when he enlisted in 1780 at the age of eighteen. Freeman served six years, two months, and two days, chiefly as the drummer for the 1st Rhode Island Regiment.

The fact that of those registered black graves, the majority were fifers and drummers who lived well into old age, may give us a possible clue as to why a stone or marker was made for these veterans. It is likely that, like Richard Cozzens, Christmas Hunt, and John Strange, these survivors embodied the living memory of the war within their communities by dressing in the uniform of the Continental Line, by marching and playing in parades, at political events, and at memorial ceremonies for many years.

The most lasting memorial to these men may be seen in the generations of their descendants and their accomplishments, detailed in the next chapter to the extent possible with surviving records. Like their Narragansett brothers in battle, those of the 1st Rhode Island Regiment had future generations in mind when they enlisted in the fight for liberty. Theirs may be said to be the first volley fired for these freedoms, even against the cannon fire of rhetoric, wrought of fear mongering and racism. They took the first ground in the long battle for their people—black and indigenous—to change the landscape of America to reflect that promise that lies within its Declaration of Independence, that all are created equal and have the inalienable right to "life, liberty, and the pursuit of happiness."

5

The Legacy of the
1st Rhode Island Regiment

HE MILITARY LEGACY LEFT BY THOSE LEADERS OF THE
1st Rhode Island Regiment spans the branches of
service from those descendants who but two generations
later fought for the Union in the Civil War, through the
conflicts that followed into modern times.

The names of those who served in the 1st Rhode Island echo through the muster rolls of the Rhode Islanders
in the Union Army. George Sears Greene, the second
cousin twice removed from Colonel Christopher Greene,
would serve with distinction in the Civil War and become
a hero in his community of Warwick, Rhode Island.

Born in humble circumstances in Apponaug as one of
nine children, George Greene found his ambitions for education and improving himself were limited in Rhode Island. It was not until he moved to New York and found

work in a mercantile store, that he met another descendant of a "soldier of the revolution" in Major Sylvanus Thayer, who recommended the young Greene to West Point Military Academy.[1] He was one of thirty-five cadets, second in his graduating class in 1823. Greene was commissioned a second lieutenant in the 3rd United States Artillery Regiment, but remained at West Point, serving as an assistant professor of mathematics, and as principal assistant of engineering, until 1827. The following year he married Mary Elizabeth Vinton, a sister of his best friend David Vinton, who also served at the academy. He resigned his commission in 1836.

As a civil engineer, Greene commenced to construct bridges, municipal sewers, and water systems in Detroit, Washington, D.C., and other cities. In New York he designed the Croton Aqueduct reservoir in Central Park and the High Bridge over the Harlem River. He also constructed six railroad lines in six different states.

With the onset of the Civil War, Greene rejoined the service. He was appointed colonel of the 60th New York Regiment, made up of militia from upstate New York. This regiment had petitioned Washington for a new commander, and the junior officers were likely dismayed when the sixty-year-old veteran arrived to take command. Despite his age and the affectionate nickname of "Pappy" given him by the common soldiers, Greene was one of the more aggressive commanders during the war.

He served as brigadier general of volunteers with General Nathaniel Banks during the campaign against Stonewall Jackson in the Shenandoah Valley. When engaged during the Battle of Cedar Mountain in northern Virginia, Greene took command of the 3rd Brigade, 2nd Division, II Corps of the Army of Virginia, after its commander, John W. Geary, was severely wounded. Greene and the troops held off a fierce rebel onslaught and provided cover for neighboring units to withdraw from the field.

Greene remained in command of the division, which was then within the XII Corps of the Army of the Potomac, which gathered at Antietam. It was here that Greene would begin to forge his legacy, with a ferocious attack on the rebel lines near Dunker Church, penetrating Jackson's defenses

George Sears Greene in 1836. (*New York Public Library*)

farther than any Union regiment had before.

After a brief leave, he again assumed command of the 3rd brigade, entering into minor skirmishes, and then taking a heavy toll of casualties during the Battle of Chancellorsville, when the brigade was in the front lines. Greene's insistence that his men make fortified trenches along the line likely saved many more lives than the five hundred and eight men who were lost to the brigade.

It was this leadership that would prove vital in the brigade's survival at Gettysburg in July 1863. Greene again had his troops construct ground fortifications at the base of Culp's Hill, a position crucial to holding the Baltimore Pike, the supply-line for the Union Army. On July 2, the brigade held off numerous attacks, with one officer recalling, "Had the breastworks not been built, and had there only been the thin line of our unprotected brigade, that line must have been swept away like leaves before the wind, by the oncoming of so heavy a mass of troops, and the [Baltimore] pike would have been reached by the enemy."[2]

Greene's own sons also served in the "war between the states." He returned home a hero and, on his death in 1899, was buried on a quiet hill above the village of Apponaug.

One of Greene's descendants, present East Greenwich town historian Bruce MacGunnigle, grew up in a household that held great pride in their ancestor's roles in the Revolutionary War. Bruce MacGunnigle's mother, Dorothy Greene MacGunnigle, and her sister, Pauline Greene Adams, were both members of the Daughters of the American Revolution. He recalls the story most often told in the family was of Eseck Burlingame, who joined Stephen Olney's Regiment in the 2nd Rhode Island at the age of sixteen in place of his older brother Nathan, who had been called to service. As there was no formal register, Eseck showed up with his musket and marched off to train with the troops. He survived, returned home, married, had twenty-one children with three wives, and lived to be ninety-one. His youngest son, Henry, born when Eseck was eighty years old, joined the Sons of the American Revolution and shared his father's longevity; he died in 1928.

MacGunnigle also has a direct connection to the 1st Rhode Island Regiment, through his grandfather's great-grandfather, private Thomas Mitchell, the fifer whose story MacGunnigle told in the introduction to his *Regimental Book Rhode Island Regiment 1781 &c.*[3]

FOR MANY OF THE BLACK AND INDIGENOUS DESCENDANTS OF those soldiers of the revolution, life was very different. The freedoms for which their ancestors had fought were not afforded to many of them after the war. Nonetheless, more than sixty years after the close of the Revolutionary

War, their names reverberate within the ranks of the "colored" regiment formed in Rhode Island for service in the Union Army.

Jeremiah Noka served in the 14th Rhode Island Artillery Battalion during the Civil War. He is mentioned in a history of the regiment from an article that portrayed the men of the regiment in the *Providence Journal*, whose journalist's depiction of race and use of political rhetoric reinforced the stereotype that the Narragansett were a people of the past: "Jeremiah Noka . . . is also a noteworthy specimen of a Rhode Islander. He is one of the purest examples which a modern intermingling of African blood has left to us of the once all-powerful tribe of Narragansetts. His fine shape, his decided Indian cast of features, his genial and winning smile, his generous expression, inevitably recall the memory of the lost Narragansett."[4]

Noka would serve in Company A of the regiment from August 1863 until his death in October 1864. He was among those enlistees moved from Dexter Training Ground in Providence after neighbors complained of a large, loud black encampment amidst the stately industrialists' homes, to Dutch Island off Newport's shore where the men built earthworks to support the sixty-four pounders that were faced out toward the opening of Narragansett Bay. His company would be among those first sent to drill at Fort Parapet, Louisiana, and then to Fort Jackson to shore up defenses on the west bank of the Mississippi River. Among the duties required were to board all vessels passing the fort, and to inspect their papers. This led to shots fired above the water, on occasion, but nothing like the danger faced by men in a close encampment surrounded by swampland. In September 1864, Captain Thomas Fry would write, "It is very sickly

here, since coming to this post in July I have lost twenty-
three men by death. I have lost twenty-eight in all."[5] Jeremiah Noka was one of these afflicted, and he died at
Fort Jackson on October 9, 1864.

Later descendants of the Perry family, whose households contained a dozen or more children each generation, would include the Perrys who served in the 14th
Rhode Island Heavy Artillery Battalion (Colored) with
Jeremiah Noka and other Narragansett men. William
Perry enlisted in November 1863 and was promoted to
sergeant the following month. He was apparently unaf-
fected by the waves of sickness that swept through the
camp, and remained with the battalion until mustered out
with the remaining troops on October 2, 1865. Daniel D.
Perry also served a lengthy term, enrolling in August 1863
and being mustered out with his cousin. Another relative
was Charles J. Quash, who enrolled the same day as
Daniel and served the same term of service.

The Perry family would contribute multiple members
of the clan to later conflicts, as the country needed warriors, including Allens, Browns, Cards, Fowlers, Halls,
Lincolns, Smiths, and other long-held names of the Narragansett people.

Among the generation of Perry descendants today are
Catherine Brown-Izzo, Nancy Brown-Garcia, and Nancy
Jo Montrond Nunez, who have worked as educators and
genealogists to keep tribal roots and history intact for future generations. Nancy Brown-Garcia writes of her lineage, "The opportunity to serve as soldiers arises
throughout our American history, whereas, the Indians assist the whites in their wars. . . . The Old Narragansett
Indian Church had engraved brass plates honoring men
of the tribe who served in the many wars. The church was
burned down by vandals and they were never replaced. I

am sad about it because all of my uncles, father, and other ancestors were on that church wall my whole life and now they are gone forever. I hope to someday replace them. It is a matter of Patriotic pride."⁶

Recognition for the indigenous peoples' contribution to the Revolutionary War has only recently been raised in the histories of the conflict. For the Narragansett, the first battle was a long struggle to regain recognition for their people. In 1978, the state of Rhode Island reached a Joint Memorandum of Understanding with the Narragansett, effectively returning some 1,800 acres of land and a cash settlement for the more than 3,200 acres the tribe had claimed based upon the 1790 settlement with the federal government. In 1983, after a lengthy legal battle, the Narragansett Tribe was formally recognized as a sovereign nation by the U.S. government.

Today on their ancestral lands, all warriors, both men and women of the tribe, are honored in a ceremony at the memorial in Great Swamp each year. The reclaiming of the site, where in 1906 the Society of Colonial Wars had erected a granite obelisk to the memory of the white soldiers killed in the battle of December 1675, was of great significance to those descendants of the indigenous warriors who had fought to protect their land and home.

Nancy Brown-Garcia writes of another long known but often overlooked memorial, named for Eugene Perry (1893–1918):

> Eugene was a very celebrated soldier of World War I, he served his country and died during the war in England. A marching band, for the Veterans of Foreign Wars assembled in Rhode Island was named in his honor and marched in several parades throughout New England and the famed Macy's Thanksgiving Day parade of New York City. The band was a colored marching band, the first of its kind in Rhode Island.

The Eugene Perry American Legion Post once located in what is now the Eugene Perry Square, located in Cranston, is an honor bestowed upon the Perry family, not just in honor of Pvt. Eugene Perry, the only son of the Supreme Grand Sachem of the National Algonquian Indian Council (circa 1826) but for all the Perrys who served for centuries in many wars. It was the first and only Native American Post granted by the state of Rhode Island . . . this was rare and monumental, an honor no one remembers but a few family members. The Post is now defunct, now just a stone represents this miraculous honor called the Eugene Perry Square. He is not known to the thousands who drive by the intersection daily. . . . I tell these facts so they will not be lost. . . . Supreme Grand Sachem Strong Horse, also known as Alfred Caesar Augustus Perry (1861–1931) lost his son in the service of his country but that did not stop the Perry spirit because his two grandchildren who were girls, both retired after long careers as military nurses. I myself joined the United States Army in 1979. Our family did not discriminate between boys or girls serving our country. I carry that Perry pride and am an avid patriot. I love my homeland where my ancestors sleep in the Earth for millenniums. I alone visit the Eugene Perry Square every year to make sure they keep up with the flags and flowers.[7]

OTHER DESCENDANTS OF SOLDIERS OF THE REVOLUTION maintained a close bond through churches or other social organizations. The Free Will Baptist Church in Warwick, Rhode Island, was largely made up of these descendants of manumitted slaves and indigenous people. The church was organized December 25, 1841, and worshiped in various places within the village of Apponaug, chiefly at the meetinghouse just north, near the High House, a popular

Left, memorial to the members of the "black soldiers of the Rhode Island Regiment" who died in the attack on the Croton River in York-town, New York. Right, monument to the Black Regiment erected in 1976 on the remnants of the battlefield in Rhode Island. (*Author*)

tavern. Among the congregation were the names of Bab-cocks and Champlins, Frys and Gardners, Hull, Holden, and Rhodes—all names well known to those who study the history of slavery in Rhode Island. At the time of the Dorr War in 1842, however, a good deal of the congrega-tion favored Governor King, and the "Law and Order" party. Many descendants of slaves within the congrega-tion were loyal Dorrites. In a letter written to Governor John Brown Francis in 1853, Susan Holden writes, "Therefore, they (the people of color) made arrange-ments to build on the plain half mile north of Apponaug village."[8] The congregation was given land along the Post Road on which to construct a church by local benefactor Stephen Budlong. Among the subscribers for the new church were John Brown Francis and his daughter Anne Brown Francis, as well as Christopher and Colonel William Rhodes of Pawtuxet, descendants of the slave owning Rhodes of the Revolutionary era. This building was dedicated in 1844.

The majority of the indigenous and formerly enslaved veterans and the regiment itself were not publicly recognized in their state of origin until the twentieth century. Public monuments to the 1st Rhode Island Regiment were erected at Patriot's Park in Portsmouth, Rhode Island, in 1976 by the Newport chapter of the NAACP's Bicentennial Commission, and in August 2005, with the commemoration of their role in the Battle of Rhode Island.[9]

The 1st Rhode Island Regiment was recognized again on February 11, 2014, with the introduction of a bill by Rhode Island congressman David Cicilline to the 113th Congress of the United States that would award the Congressional Gold Medal to the members of the 1st Rhode Island Regiment collectively, "in recognition of their dedicated service during the Revolutionary War." While HR 4505 died in Congress, Rep. Cicilline reintroduced the bill in January 2015, as HR 363, and this was assigned to committee for further discussion.

Today, the legacy of the 1st Rhode Island Regiment is largely kept alive through historical writings, videos, and military reenactment groups.

Appendix A

List of Officers and Enlisted Soldiers of Euro-
American Descent in the 1st Rhode Island Regiment
(From Anthony Walker, *So Few the Brave*)
d.=discharged des.=deserted? r.=reassigned?

January 1777–January 1781

COMMANDING OFFICERS

Lt. Col. Adam Comstock
Lt. Col. Archibald Crary
Major Ebenezer Flagg
Col. Christopher Greene
Lt. Col. Samuel Ward

CAPTAINS

Joseph Arnold
Thomas Arnold
Zephaniah Brown
Thomas Cole
John S. Dexter
John Holden Jr.
Elijajh Lewis
Edward Slocum
Silas Talbot
John Topham
Jonathan Wallen

LIEUTENANTS

Chandler Burlingame
William Davis (1777–d. 1778)
Daniel Dexter
Samuel Hicks (1776–r. 1778)
Elias Hull (1776–r. 1778)
David Johnson (1777–d. 1780)
Charles Pierce (1777–r. 1779)

Enoch Stanton (1777–r. 1779)
Joseph Whitmarsh (1776–r. 1778)
Micah Whitmarsh (1775–r. 1778)

ENSIGNS

Elias Blanchard (1777–1780)
Stephen Briggs (1777–1778)
Gideon Casey (1777–1778)
John Chapman (1777–1780)
John Cooke (1777–1780)
Joseph Cornell (1777–1779)
Griffin Greene (1777–1778)
Jonathan Hazard (1777–1778)
Simon Smith (1777–1778)
Richard Springer (1777)

STAFF

Daniel Dexter (Feb. 1780)
John Holden (1777–1780)

First Rhode Island Continentals (Olney's Battalion)
January 1781–November 1783

COMMANDING OFFICERS

Col. Christopher Greene (d. May 1781)
Lt. Col. Jeremiah Olney (1775–1783)

MAJORS

John S. Dexter (1775–1783) nine battle stars
Ebenezer Flagg (d. May 1781)
Coggeshall Olney (1775–1783) eleven battle stars

CAPTAINS

William Allen (1775–1783)
Zephaniah Brown (1776–1783)
Thomas Cole (1775–r. 1782)
Daniel Dexter (1777–1783)
John Holden (1776–1783)

Thomas Hughes (1776–1783)
William Humphrey (1775–r. 1783)
Dutee Jerauld (1776–r. 1782)
Ebenezer Macomber (1776–1783)
Stephen Olney (1775–r. 1782)
Benjamin Peckham (1777–1783)
David Sayles (1776–1783)

LIEUTENANTS

Chandler Burlingame (1776–1783)
William Ennis (1781–1783)
John M. Greene (1780–1783)
Jeremiah Greenman (1780–1783)
John Hubbard (1777–1783)
Oliver Jenckes (1776–1782)
Joseph Mashbury (1780–1783)
William Pratt (1777–1783)
John Rogers (1777–1783)
Henry Shearman (1777–1783)
Benjamin Sherburne (1777–1783)
John Welch (1782–1783)
Joseph Wheaton (1781–1783)

ENSIGNS

Rueben Johnson (1781–des. 1782)
Ephraim Kirby (1776–1783)

ENLISTED MEN 1781–1783

Pardon Abbott—Cranston
Peter Barrows—Cumberland
Jotham Bemus—NY—enlisted in East Greenwich
William Bennet—Providence
Benjamin Bickford—Johnston—enlisted at Morristown, 1780
Benjamin Blanchard—Scituate
Thomas Bond—Providence
Joseph T. Brown—New London—enlisted at Warwick
Edward Butterick

John Chadwick—Newport—enlisted at Tiverton
John Chilson—North Providence/Smithfield
Daniel Collins—Scituate
Hosea Crandle—Hopkinton—enlisted at Tiverton
Charles Crosbee Worcester/Smithfield
Emer Dailey—Johnston
Benajah Davis—Westerly
William Davis—Westerly
Thomas Dexter—Rehoboth—enlisted at Warwick
Fairman Dye—Tiverton
John Earl—Tiverton
David Edwards—Swansey
John Fields—Cumberland
Abel Gibbs—Coventry—enlisted at East Greenwich
Simeon Goodspeed—Foster
Richard Grant—Bristol
George Greene—Foster—enlisted at Providence
James Greene—Coventry
James Greene 2nd—Cranston—enlisted at Glocester
Howland Greenhill—Little Compton
Benjamin Hall—Hopkinton
Nicholas Hart—Washington County
Jabez Hawkins—Providence
Benjamin Jackson—Newport
Uriah Jones—Smithfield
Hugh Kennedy—Voluntown—enlisted at West Greenwich
Daniel Lake—Tiverton
Barney Matts—Newport
Charles McAfferty—enlisted at Bristol
Ruben Nichols—Coventry—enlisted at East Greenwich
James Ogg—Pennsylvania—enlisted at Providence
Moses Perkins—Groton, Conn.—enlisted at New London
Jesse Pierce—Rehoboth—enlisted at Providence
Welcom Pigsly—Mendham, Ma.—enlisted at Glocester
James Pollard—Taunton—enlisted at Coventry
Abraham Rose—Sandwich, Mass.—enlisted at Tiverton

John Saunders—Smithfield
Joshua Smith—Westerly
Durfee Springer—Newport—enlisted at Tiverton
Thomas Stafford—Coventry—enlisted at East Greenwich
Jeremiah Stone—Providence
John Sweet—Glocester
Samuel Thompson—Boston—enlisted at South Kingstown
Rhodes Tucker—Cranston—enlisted at Warwick
Ruben Turtolot—Glocester—enlisted at Providence
Stutely Wescott—Washington County—enlisted at Providence
Nathan West—Newport
John Wilbour—Little Compton
Silvester Woodman—Little Compton

Appendix B

Indigenous Rhode Islanders Who Served
in the Revolutionary War
(from Eric G. Grundset, *Forgotten Patriots*)
Entries provide name, town, and year of enlistment, or
discharge, along with other available information.

James Anthony—discharged May 1781
John Anthony—1st R.I. Regiment
Joseph Anthony—died in service 1777
Samuel Apis
Aaron Benedick—Charlestown, 1777
John Brown—Charlestown, 1777
John Brown—Johnston, 1777
Primus Brown—enslaved man of Gideon Brown
Jeremiah Caesar—Johnston, 1777
Solomon Caesar—1st and 2nd R.I. Regiments
Emphraim Charles—Charlestown, 1777
John Charles—1st R.I. Regiment
Stephen Charles—1st and 2nd R.I. Regiments. Died December 15, 1781
George Chunks
Mingo Cook
Joseph Cornette
William Cory—North Kingstown
Jophrey Couchup
Joseph Couchup
Peter Couchup—served on sloop *Independence*
Elisha Coy
Toby Coy
Jacob Davids
Peleg Dexter
Peter Dimon (Dimond)
Caesar Finch—Coventry—Ist and 2nd R.I. Regiments
Benjamin Fitch

Winsor Fry—East Greenwich, 1777
Henry Hazard—1st and 2nd R.I. Regiments
Pharoah Hazard—1777
Christopher Henry—Charlestown, 1777
Daniel Henry—Charlestown, 1777
Gideon Henry—1st and 2nd R.I. Regiments
John Henry—drummer, 1st and 2nd R.I. Regiments
Silas Henry—Charlestown, 1777
Benjamin Inow
Jonathan Jeffers
Daniel Jeffrey
Joseph Jeffrey—Charlestown, 1777
Edward Jones
Anthony Mocan
Solomon Ned
James Nocake
John Nocake—1st R.I. Regiment
Joseph Nocake—1st and 2nd R.I. Regiments
Josiah Nocake
Daniel Pace
James Parr
John Pery (Perry)—seaman on ship *Alfred*
Jabez Primus—Westerly, 1777
Moses Skeezouchs
Daniel Skesuck—Block Island, 1777
Jonathan Spywood—1st R.I. Regiment
Samson Spywood—Warwick, 1777
Aaron Suckkush—Little Compton, 1777
Simon Sucknesh—Cray's Regiment
Aaron Sunchiman
Natus Suronded
Peter Toby
James Updike—fifer, North Kingstown
Cato Varnum—slave of James Varnum
Elija Waggs
Simon Waggs

John Wampy—1st and 2nd R.I. Regiments
Samuel Wampy
George Weaver—Charlestown, 1777
Benoni West—Warwick, 1777
Ishmael West—Warwick, 1777

Also:
Cato Brown and Sambo Brown served in regiments in Connecticut.
Anthony Jeremiah, "a Narragansett Man," served in Connecticut as well. He was dubbed "Red Jerry" by the white soldiers of the regiment.

Appendix C

Documentation of Slaves

1. "A List of Negroe Slaves Inlisted into the Continental Battalions and to Whom They Belonged," 1778 (from Sidney S. Rider, *An Historical Inquiry Concerning the Attempt to Raise a Regiment of Slaves in Rhode Island During the War of the Revolution*)

Rider used this incomplete list to foster his argument that the recruitment of slaves was nearly nonexistent among the wider population of slaves in the state. The list does not include those slaves given over by their masters in place of sons or other relatives, nor does it include those slaves who escaped their masters to enlist, or slaves who enlisted after 1778. The list does seem to indicate that recruitment went much past the date of June 1 decreed by the Assembly after the initial Act offering freedom in exchange for service.

DATE	SLAVE	MASTER	PLACE
Feb. 25	Cuff Greene	James Greene	Providence
	Dick Champlin	Stephen Champlin	S. Kingstown
	Jack Champlin	Stephen Champlin	S. Kingstown
Mar. 6	Titus Peirce	William Peirce	East Greenwich
	Africa Burke	James Burke	Providence
	Sigby Talbot	Silas Talbot	Providence
Mar. 31	Backus Hazard	Robert Hazard	S. Kingstown
April 2	Jack Fones	Daniel Fones	N. Kingstown
3	Cudjo Carpenter	Heirs of Ann Carpenter	S. Kingstown
3	Caesar Wells	James Wells Jr.	Hopkington
3	Cuff Gardner	Christopher Gardner	S. Kingstown
3	Sharper Gardner	Benj. Gardner	S. Kingstown
3	Prince Hammond	William Hammond	N. Kingstown
3	Quam Tanner	Joshua Tanner	Hopkington
3	Prince Bent	John Bent	Hopkington

4	Nat Wicks	John Wicks	Warwick
11	York Champlin	Robert Champlin	S. Kingstown
14	Boston Wilbour	John Wilbour	Little Compton
14	John Burroughs	William Burroughs	Newport
14	Ebenaezer Richmond	Peres Richmond	Little Compton
20	Priamus Brown	Gideon Brown	Johnston
21	Cato Vernon	William Vernon	Newport
23	Isaac Rodman	Daniel Rodman	S. Kingstown
24	Briton Saltonstall	Dudley Saltonstall	Westerly
May 8	James Clark	Gideon Clark	S. Kingstown
8	Mintel Gardner	Henry Gardner	S. Kingstown
8	Moses Updike	Lodowick Updike	N. Kingstown
8	Caesar Updike	Lodowick Updike	N. Kingstown
8	Garret Perry	Benjamin Perry	S. Kingstown
8	Sampson Saunders	Heirs of Stephen Saunders	Westerly
8	Ruttee Gardner	Nicholas Gardner	Exeter
8	Ebenezer Gray	Samuel Gray	Little Compton
8	Prince Randal	Henry Randal	Cranston
22	Thomas Nichols	Benjamin Nichols	Warwick
22	Pero Greene	Philip Greene	Warwick
22	Jack Greene	Phillip Greene	Warwick
27	Pero Mowry	Daniel Mowry Jr.	Smithfield
28	Juba Smith	Josiah Smith	Bristol
28	Caesar Sheldon	Palmer Sheldon	S. Kingstown
29	Bristol Rhodes	Joseph Rhodes	Cranston
29	Fortune Watson	Samuel Watson	N. Kingstown
June 1	Query Sweeting	Job Sweeting	Providence
1	Jack Minturn	William Minturn	Newport
6	Caesar Rose	John Rose.	S. Kingstown
6	Edward Rose	John Rose	S. Kingstown
6	Peter Hazard	Rob't Hazard s/o Richard	S. Kingstown
6	Priamus Babcock	Samuel Babcock	Hopkington
6	David Potter	Caleb Potter	Cranston
12	Jack Coddington	John Coddington	Newport
17	Caesar Harris	Andrew Harris	Cranston
18	Sharper Champlin	Christopher Champlin	Newport

4. Africa Burke
5. Frank Bowen
6. Newport Champlin
7. Jack Coddington
8. William Greene
9. Juno Greene
10. Cato Wm. Greene
11. Cato R. Greene
12. Minters Gardiner
13. Prosper Gorton
14. Prince Torqusham
15. Sampson Hazard
16. Pero Morey
17. Titus Pierce
18. Prime Rhodes
19. Mingo Robinson
20. Prime Sayles
21. Brittain Salton(stall)
22. Harry Tabor
23. Boston Wilber
24. Nathan Wickes
25. Cudgo Champlin
26. Jude Smith
27. Cuff Slade
28. Prince Rodman
29. Bristol Arnold

Appendix D

Rhode Islanders Who Departed from New York
on British Vessels During the Evacuation, 1783
From the "Inspection Roll of Negroes" reprinted in
The Black Loyalist Directory

BOOK I

Jeremy Dyer, 20, Tall and stout—formerly slave to Samuel Dyer, Rhode Island, left him with the troops 4 years ago. Registered on the ship *Ladys Adventure*, leaving New York for England. (p. 11)

Keatie Dyer, 25, stout mulatto wench formerly servant to Dyer—Rhode Island. "Left that place with the troops six years ago." (p. 13)

Jacob Wanton, 35, ordinary man, . . . formerly slave to Latham Thurston, Rhode Island "Left him with the troops four years past by Proclamation." Register of ship *Anne*, bound for Port Roseway.

Nancy Mumford, 21, stout wench, free as per bill of sale of her mother from Mrs. Mumford, Rhode Island to her father Bristol. (p. 31)

John Tucker, 18,—formerly slave of Captain Smith, Newport. Registered on ship *Grace* bound for Port Roseway.

Hana Hazard, 36, likely wench. "Born free to a certainty in Rhode Island" . . . also Ben Hazard, 11, fine boy (pp. 38–39)

Fonlove Jackson, 25, likely wench, M (on her own bottom). Free wench born in Rhode Island . . . also Dinah Jackson, 9, fine girl . . . Ned Jackson, 6, fine boy. All above on ship *Providence* bound for Port Roseway. (p. 39)

Samuel Warner, 36, ordinary fellow, formerly slave to William Warner, Warwick, Rhode Island. "Left him about six years past." Registered on ship *Mary*. (p. 41)

Jack Rogers, 50, stout man—left free by his master James Rogers, Newport, Rhode Island, who died 5 years before the war. (p. 45)

Jemima Bull, 26, slender wench, formerly slave to Asa Bull, left him with the British troops in 1779. Also Philip Bull, 13, Millia Bull, 6, Cazar Bull, 1. Registered on the ship *Tree Briton* bound for Port Roseway. (p. 52)

Pompey Hadin, 27, stout fellow, cuts in each cheek, formerly slave to Josias Lyndon, Rhode Island. Left him 4 years past. Registered on ship *Tree Briton* bound for Port Roseway. (p. 53)

Cuff Potter, 53, M (on his own bottom), formerly slave to Ralph Potter, Rhode Island; left him in the year 1779 with the British troops. Registered on ship *Symmetry* bound for St. Johns. (p. 54)

Pompey Wanton, 25, squat fellow, formerly slave to Stephen Wanton, Rhode Island, "left him at the evacuation of said place." Registered on the ship *Ann* bound for St. John's River. (p. 64)

Fanny Mosely, 27, strong, ugly wench formerly slave to William Mosely, Rhode Island. "Left him four years past and joined the British troops." Also Tommy Mosely, 1, B. born within the British Lines. Registered on the ship *Elizabeth* bound for St. John's River. (p. 67)

John Potter, 25, stout fellow, formerly slave to Robert Potter of Rhode Island; left him 5 years ago. Registered on ship *Montague* bound for St. John's River. (p. 70)

Pater Packer, 40, [stout fellow] with one arm, —"Formerly the property of Thomas Parker of Providence, Rhode Island, whom he says gave him his freedom & produces Gen. Birch's Certificate." Registered on ship *Peggy* bound for St. John's River. (p. 79)

Rose Williams, 28, stout wench—says she is free . . . came from Rhode Island six years ago. Also Henry Williams, 1, "sickly child," son to Rose . . . born within the British Lines. Registered on ship *L'Abondance* bound for Port Roseway. (p. 83)

Jenny Toney, 52, worn out. Formerly property of Daniel Underwood, Connecticut, Rhode Island; free by Bill of Sale.

Registered on the ship *L'Abondance* bound for Port Roseway. (p. 107)

Amos Carrey, 45, stout fellow, formerly property of Mrs. Col.
Carrey of Newport; left her 7 (years ago). Registered on
the ship *L'Abondance* bound for Port Roseway. (p. 108)

George Barnes, 47, feeble fellow, goes as Cook to the Ship.
Says he is a free man; produces a Certificate date 1770
from John Davis of Newport, Rhode Island, Justice of the
Peace. Also Rachel, 7, fine child. Daughter to George
Barnes. Registered on ship *Anne & Elizabeth* bound for
[Spithead & Germany]. (p. 121)

Bridget Wanton, 22, "stout little woman and small girl 5
years old. [Formerly the property] of Colonel Joseph Wanton of Rhode Island who at his death left (her) free." Registered on the ship *William* transport bound for Abbaco.
(p. 129)

Diana Carden, 24, ordinary wench, formerly slave to Richard
Burke, Rhode Island; left him 7 years ago. Registered on
the ship *Montague* bound for St. John's. (p. 135)

BOOK II. SEPTEMBER–NOVEMBER 1783

Ming, 26, stout fellow—formerly slave to Mr. Reynolds,
Rhode Island Government; left with troops evacuating
that Garrison. Registered on the ship *Michael* bound for
Annapolis. (p. 155)

Ben Freebody, 35, ordinary fellow, formerly slave to Samuel
Freebody, Newport, Rhode Island; left him 7 years ago.
Registered on ship *Cato* bound for Annapolis Royal. (p.
162)

Rose Wansworth, 30, "[stout] wench, 2 children 12 & 5 years
of age. Formerly slave to Daniel Russel of Newport,
Rhode Island; left him 7 years ago." Registered on Sloop
Skuldham bound for Annapolis Royal. (p. 163)

Lucy Johnson, 25, ordinary wench. Says she was born free
in Rhode Island. Registered on Brig *Elijah* bound for Port
Mattoon. (p. 171)

Patience Jackson, 23, very likely [wench], says she was born free in Rhode Island . . . Registered on Brig *Elijah* bound for Port Mattoon. (p. 171)

Betty Westerfield, 28, stout wench, . . . Born free at Rhode Island. Also Phyllis, 40, stout wench, . . . Born free at Rhode Island. Registered on the Brig *Jenney* bound for Port Mattoon. (p. 184)

James Annie, 39, stout fellow . . . formerly slave to John Annie, Rhode Island. "left him in 1779."

Arthur Boler, 34, stout fellow. Formerly slave to Medcalfe Bowler, Portsmouth, Rhode Island; [left him in 1781]. Also, Phebe {Boler} 35, ordinary wench. Says she was born free.{Portsmouth, Rhode Island}, and Betsy {boler} likely girl. {Says she was born free . . . Registered on the ship *Nisbet* bound for Port Mattoon. (pp. 189–190)

BOOK III

Rose Gozeman, 24, stout wench . . . Formerly slave to John Easton, Rhode Island, left him about 4 years ago. Registered on the Brig *Concord*. (p. 205)

Cato Rogers, 44 years, stout fellow . . . Formerly slave to William Rogers of Newport, Rhode Island; left him 5 years ago. Registered on board the *Diannah* bound for Port Mattoon.

Notes

ONE: THE ORIGINS OF THE 1ST RHODE ISLAND REGIMENT

1. Famously named for its wooden sign of a cluster of grapes that hung above the door. The sign resided for many years in the Rhode Island Historical Society.

2. Oliver Payson Fuller, *The History of Warwick, R.I.* (Providence: Burlingame & Co., 1875), 118.

3. Robert Middlekauff, *The Glorious Cause: The American Revolution 1763–1789*, revised and expanded edition (London: Oxford University Press, 2005), 310.

4. Henry A.L. Brown, *From Occupastuxet to Red Bank: A History of Cole's Farm* (East Greenwich, R.I.: Dark Entry Press, 2014), 10.

5. Middlekauff, *The Glorious Cause*, 313.

6. William Humphrey, "A Journal Made in the Year 1775–1776," from *Rhode Islanders Record the Revolution: The Journals of William Humphrey and Zuriel Waterman* (Providence: Rhode Island Publications Society, 1984), 32–33.

7. Middlekauff, *The Glorious Cause*, 313.

8. Pension File for Lieutenant Robert Rogers, N0. S21455, *Selected Records from Revolutionary War Pension Files*, NARA Microfilm M805, Roll 701.

9. Richard Bray and Paul Bushnell (eds). *Diary of a Common Soldier in the American Revolution 1775–1783, An Annotated Edition of the Military Journal of Jeremiah Greenman* (DeKalb: Northern Illinois University Press, 1978), 81.

10. Ibid., 81–82.

11. Olney Narrative, Shepley Papers, Rhode Island Historical Society, 15.

12. W. C. Nell, *Colored Patriots of the American Revolution* (Boston, 1855), 126–131.

13. Greenman (Bray and Bushnell, eds.), *Diary of a Common Soldier in the American Revolution*, 82.

14. Ibid., 88.

15. Bartlett, *Records of the State of Rhode Island and Providence Plantations*, vol. 8: 641.

TWO: FROM SLAVES TO SOLDIERS

1. Sidney S. Rider, *An Historical Inquiry concerning the Attempt to Raise a Regiment of Slaves in Rhode Island*, Rhode Island Historical Tracts 10 (1880), 11.

2. Gary Nash, *The Forgotten Fifth: African Americans in the Age of Revolution* (Cambridge, Mass.: Harvard University Press, 2006), 24–27.

3. Gerald Horne, *The Counter-Revolution of 1776: Slave Resistance and the Origins of the United States of America* (New York: New York University Press, 2014), 237.

4. As a Virginian, Washington was acutely aware of the recurrent fear of uprising among the plantation owners of his colony. The general was no doubt aware of Great Britain's use of slave warriors in their struggles to retain islands of its empire, as well as the flood of slaves who escaped the Carolinas to Spanish Florida with the promise of freedom. The European power would form regiments of these former slaves, leading to fear of an invasion of the American colonies by slave-led troops under a Spanish flag. See Gerald Horne's *Counter-Revolution of 1776* for a fuller understanding of these tensions in the southern colonies before the war.

5. Entry of June 30, 1777, from *Diary of Frederick MacKenzie Giving a Daily Narrative of his Military Service as an Officer of the Regiment of Royal Welch Fusiliers During the Years 1775–1781 in Massachusetts Rhode Island and New York* (Cambridge, Mass.: Harvard University Press, 1930), 145. See also Christian McBurney, *Spies in Revolutionary Rhode Island* (Charleston, S.C.: History Press, 2014), 73.

6. Rhode Island, Historical Society, Revolutionary War Papers, MSS 673 SG2 Box 1 F. 52.

7. Patrick Rael, *Eighty Eight Years: The Long Death of Slavery in the United States 1777–1865* (Athens: University of Georgia Press, 2015), 57.

8. Ira Berlin, *The Long Emancipation: The Demise of Slavery in the United States* (Cambridge, Mass.: Harvard University Press, 2015), 54.

9. Lorenzo Johnston Greene, *The Negro in Colonial New England 1620–1776* (New York: Columbia University Press, 1942), 86–89.

10. William D. Piersen, *Black Yankees: The Development of an Afro-American Subculture in Eighteenth Century New England* (Amherst: University of Massachusetts Press, 1988), 44.

11. Ibid., 105.

12. See Robert A. Geake, *Historic Rhode Island Farms* (Charleston, S.C.: History Press, 2012), 24–25.

13. Greene, *Negro in Colonial New England*, 105.

14. Wilkins Updike, *The History of the Narragansett Church*, vol. 1 (Boston: Merrymount Press, 1907), 224.

15. Peter Charles Hoffer, *Cry Liberty: The Great Stono River Rebellion of 1730* (London: Oxford University Press, 2010), 23.

16. Ibid., 42.

17. Ibid., 170.

18. Updike, *The History of the Narrangansett Church*, vol. 1.

19. Early Records of the City of Providence: Will Book No. 2, 243–244.

20. Greene, *Negroes in Colonial New England*, 175.

21. William L. Ransey, *The Yamasee War: A Study of Culture, Economy and Conflict in the Colonial South* (Lincoln: University of Nebraska Press, 2008), 162, 163.

22. Horne, *The Counter-Revolution of 1776*, 88.

23. Hoffer, *Cry Liberty*, 67–68.

24. Ibid., 84.

25. For a compelling account of this tragic affair, I would recommend to the reader Hoffer's *Cry Liberty: The Great Stono Slave Rebellion of 1739*. Hoffer's argument rings true with what we know today of the effect of "mob mentality" on groups of individuals that, even in times of celebration, can lead to violence.

26. Horne, *The Counter Revolution of 1776*, 167.

27. Ibid., 167.

28. James N. Arnold, *Vital Records of Rhode Island*, vol. 12, *Revolutionary Rolls and Newspapers* (Providence: Narragansett Historical Publishing, 1891), 437.

29. Horne, *The Counter Revolution of 1776*, 163.

30. James Corbett David, *Dunmore's New World* (Charlottesville: University Press of Virginia, 2015), 97.

31. Ibid., 105.

32. Mackenzie, *Diary of Frederick MacKenzie*, vol. 2, 326.

33. John Russell Bartlett, ed., *Records of the State of Rhode Island and Providence Plantation in New England* (Providence: Cooke, Jackson & Co., 1864), vol. 9: 493–510.

34. Woody Holton, *Black Americans in the Revolutionary Era: A Brief History with Documents* (Boston: Bradford/St. Martins, 2009), 68–70.

35. Ibid.

36. Rev. Frederic Denison, *Westerly Rhode Island and its Witnesses, For Two Hundred and Fifty Years 1626–1876* (Providence: J.A. Reid, 1878), 119.

37. It is telling that listed within the three volumes of "Inspection Rolls of Negroes" some three thousand souls who left New York City aboard British vessels in the summer and fall of 1783, contain but forty-nine Rhode Islanders, eighteen men, eighteen women, and thirteen children, both former slaves and free blacks among them. See Graham R. Hodges, ed., *The Black Loyalist Directory* (New York: Garland, 1996).

38. Henry Wiencek writes in his *Imperfect God: George Washington, His Slaves, and the Creation of America* (New York, Farrar, Straus and Giroux, 2003) most convincingly that Valley Forge commands a place in the history of emancipation, and that emancipation at the time of recruitment for a black regiment "was gaining momentum as a goal in itself." See also Alfred F. Young and Gregory Nobles, *Whose American Revolution Was It?* (New York: New York University Press, 2011).

39. Rider, *An Historical Inquiry Concerning the Attempt to Raise a Regiment of Slaves By Rhode Island During the War of the Revolution*, Rhode Island Historical Tract No. 10 (Providence: Rhode Island Historical Society, 1880), 11–12.

40. Letter from Nicholas Cooke to George Washington, February 23, 1778, as printed in the *Colonial Records of Rhode Island*, vol. 8 (Providence: Anthony Allen, 1864), 526.

41. William Greene was elected the second governor of the state in May 1778 after Nicholas Cooke stepped down.

42. Bartlett, ed., *Records of the State of Rhode Island and Providence Plantation in New England*, vol. 8: 561.

43. Benjamin Quarles, *The Negro in the American Revolution* (Chapel Hill: University of North Carolina Press, 1961), 59.

44. See Eric G. Grundset, ed., *Forgotten Patriots: African American and American Indian Patriots in the Revolutionary War* (Washington, D.C.: National Society of Daughters of the American Revolution, 2008), 224–232.

45. See the extensive footnotes in Christian McBurney's *Jailed for Preaching* (South Kingstown, R.I.: Pettaquamscutt Historical Society, 2006, 31–48) for a listing of South County sources on slaves who served in the Continental Army.

46. Grundset, ed., *Forgotten Patriots*, 207.

47. Carl R. Woodward, *Plantation in Yankeeland* (Wickford, R.I.: Cocumscussoc Association, 1971), 139.

48. Deloss Willliam Love, *Samsom Occom and the Christian Indians of New England* (Boston: Pilgrim Press, 1899), 335–367.

49. Princess Redwing, from notes for an address before the Woonsocket Council of the DAR, December, 1940. From the archives of the Tomaquag Museum, Exeter, Rhode Island.

50. "His father" refers to Miantonomo, a great sachem of the Narragansett who was murdered by the Mohegan under Connecticut authority in 1641.

51. Letter from Nancy Brown-Garcia to author, March 14, 2016.

52. East Greenwich, R.I. See Greenman (Bray and Bushnell, eds.), *Diary of a Common Soldier in the American Revolution*, 113.

53. Ibid., 114.

THREE: BATTLES, BLOOD, AND BROTHERHOOD

1. Mackenzie, *Diary of Frederick Mackenzie*, vol. 1: 178.
2. Ibid., 185.
3. Ibid., 252.
4. Ibid., 268.
5. Christian M. McBurney, *The Rhode Island Campaign: The First French and American Operation in the Revolutionary War* (Yardley, Pa.: Westholme Publishing, 2011), 101–102.
6. MacKenzie, *Diary of Frederick Mackenzie*, vol. 2: 341.
7. Patrick Conley, "The Battle of Rhode Island, 29 August 1778: A Victory for the Patriots," *Rhode Island History* 62, no. 3 (Fall 2004), 54.
8. Ibid., 55.
9. Ibid., 55.
10. Ibid.
11. Samuel Greene Arnold, *The Centennial Celebration of the Battle of Rhode Island*, Historical Tract No. 8 (Rhode Island Historical Society, 1878), 15.
12. McBurney, *The Rhode Island Campaign*, 170.
13. Ibid., 177.
14. Letter to Governor Greene from General Sullivan dated August 29, 1778, quoted in Rider, *An Historical Inquiry*, 22.
15. Arnold, *The Centennial Celebration of The Battle of Rhode Island*, 27.
16. Ibid., 60.
17. John Ward, *A Memoir of Lieutenant-Colonel Samuel Ward, First Rhode Island Regiment, Army of the American Revolution; With a Genealogy of the Ward Family* (New York: Privately printed, 1875), 13.
18. McBurney, *The Rhode Island Campaign*, 188.
19. Bruce C. MacGunnigle, *Regimental Book Rhode Island Regiment for 1781 &c.* (East Greenwich, R.I.: Society of the Sons of the American Revolution, 2011), xviii.
20. Quoted in Rider, *An Historical Inquiry*, 21–22.
21. Joseph Plumb Martin (George F. Sheer, ed.), *Private Yankee Doodle, Being a Narrative of Some of the Adventures, Dangers, and Sufferings of a Revolutionary Soldier* (Boston: Little, Brown, 1962), 68.
22. Benjamin Cowell, *Spirit of '76 in Rhode Island: or Sketches of the Efforts of the Government and People in the War of Revolution* (Boston, 1850), 312.
23. Edward Field, ed., *Diary of Colonel Israel Angell 1778–1781* (Providence: Preston and Rounds, 1899), xii.
24. Martin, *Private Yankee Doodle*, 184.
25. Ibid., 284.
26. Bartlett, ed., *Records of the Colony of Rhode Island and Providence Plantations* 1776– 1779, vol. 8 (Providence: Anthony Allen, 1864), 579.

27. Bartlett, ed., *Records of the Colony of Rhode Island and Providence Plantation 1780–*, vol. 9: 175–177.

28. Letter from the Marquis de Lafayette to Colonel Christopher Greene, July 28, 1780. Transcribed by Henry A. L. Brown from the papers of Thomas Greene. Private collection.

29. See Rider, *An Historical Inquiry*, 26.

30. Lincoln Diamant, "When a Black Unit Battled the British," *New York Times*, May 12, 1996.

31. Maureen Alice Taylor, *Runaways, Deserters, and Notorious Villains from Rhode Island Newspapers*, vol. 1: 108–111.

32. Letter from General George Washington to Governor Nicholas Cooke of Rhode Island, sent from headquarters at Morristown, New Jersey, 31 January 1777. Printed in *Autograph Letters and Documents of George Washington now in Rhode Island Collections* (Providence: State of Rhode Island, 1932), 36.

33. Quarles, *The Negro in the American Revolution*, 71–72.

34. I did not want to burden the narrative with the argument begun by Sidney S. Rider in his *An Historical Inquiry into the 1st Rhode Island Regiment* and continued in Daniel M. Popek's massive history, *"'They Fought Bravely, But Were Unfortunate': The True Story of Rhode Island's 'Black Regiment' and the Failure of Segregation in Rhode Island's Continental Line, 1777–1783* (Bloomington, Ind.: AuthorHouse, 2015) yet the record clearly disputes their statements. The DAR listing in Eric Grundset's *Forgotten Patriots* shows that but twenty-six of these former slaves, indigenous men, and men of mixed race, deserted the regiment during the eight years of war. At least twelve were reinstated and served out their term of enlistment.

35. Grundset, *Forgotten Patriots*, 119.

36. Quarles, *The Negro in the American Revolution*, 73.

37. Ibid., 79.

38. Wiencek, *An Imperfect God*, 201.

39. Letter to Colonel Samuel Ward from Colonel Christopher Greene, 16 April 1781. Transcribed by Henry A.L. Brown from the papers of Thomas E. Greene.

40. Nell, *Colored Patriots of the American Revolution*, 130.

41. See Fuller, *The History of Warwick, R.I.*, footnote comprised of Lee's statements, 120.

42. Marcius S. Raymond, "Colonel Christopher Greene," *Magazine of History* 23 (September–October 1916), 144–147. See also Popek, *"'They Fought Bravely, But Were Unfortunate,'"* 493.

43. MacGunnigle, *Regimental Book Rhode Island Regiment for 1781*, 59–79.

44. Thatcher, *A Military Journal*, 248.

45. Anthony Walker, *So Few the Brave* (Newport, R.I.: Seafield Press, 1981), 78.
46. Thatcher, *A Military Journal*, 255.
47. Greenman (Bray and Bushnell, eds.), *Diary of a Common Soldier in the American Revolution*, 208.
48. Ibid.
49. Richard M. Ketchum, *Victory at Yorktown: The Campaign that Won the Revolution* (New York: Henry Holt, 2004), 94.
50. Middlekauf, *The Glorious Cause*, 492.
51. Ketchum, *Victory at Yorktown*, 218.
52. Middlekauf, *The Glorious Cause*, 588.
53. Gary Nash, *The Forgotten Fifth: African Americans in the Age of Revolution* (Cambridge, Mass.: Harvard University Press, 2006), 35–37.
54. Martin, *Private Yankee Doodle*, 241.
55. Samuel Greene Arnold, *History of the State of Rhode Island* (New York: D. Appleton, 1874), vol. 2: 474–475.
56. Ketchum, *Victory at Yorktown*, 239.
57. Don Glickstein, *After Yorktown: The Final Struggle for American Independence* (Yardley, Pa.: Westholme, 2016), 20.
58. Ibid., 21.
59. Ibid., 479.
60. MacGunnigle, *Book Register, Rhode Island Regiment 1781*, 55–79.
61. Today the burial site is the park in Washington Square. As Daniel Popek points out in his massive work on the regiment (*"They Fought Bravely, But Were Unfortunate"*), there is as yet no monument to the Rhode Islanders buried there.
62. The order, signed March 8, 1782, was printed in the *Providence Gazette* the following day.
63. Letter to George Washington from Jeremiah Olney, dated March 19, 1782, Founding Era Collection, University of Virginia.
64. Letter to George Washington from Jeremiah Olney, August 4, 1782, Founding Era Collection, University of Virginia.
65. Letter of Nathanael Greene to General Thomas Sumter, May 17, 1781, *Papers of Nathanael Greene*, vol. 8 (RIHS, 1995), 278–279.
66. Letter from Governor John Martin to Gen. Greene, March 17, 1781, see Gregory D. Massey and James R. Piecuch, eds., *General Nathanael Greene and the American Revolution in the South* (Columbia: University of South Carolina Press, 2012), 244.
67. Despite this public stance during his lifetime, Greene as commander did authorize pay in the form of captured southern slaves for reenlisted troops, and on the same day that South Carolina rejected his request for a regiment of manumitted slaves, they awarded the general the gift of the Mulberry Grove Plantation, whereby Greene

became owner of an estimated 350 slaves. At the close of the war, Greene's debts were such that he deemed it unaffordable to manumit the population, though his plantation ultimately failed. See Gerald M. Carbone, *Nathanael Greene: A Biography of the American Revolution* (New York: Palgrave Macmillan, 2008), 194–195, 218–219.

68. MacGunnigle, *Regimental Book Rhode Island Regiment*, 83.

69. Arnold, *History of the State of Rhode Island*, vol. 2, 497.

70. Rider, *An Historical Inquiry*, 64.

FOUR: THE AFTERMATH OF WAR

1. See the foreword to Bruce MacGunnigle's *Regimental Book Rhode Island Regiment* for a fuller and more personal account of Mitchell's service. My thanks to Elizabeth Gates and her husband, also descendants, and caretakers of the property, for their welcome and guidance in finding Major Mitchell's grave.

2. See Index of Revolutionary War Pension Applications in the National Archives, Bicentennial Edition (Washington, D.C.: National Genealogical Society, 1976), 497.

3. The debate concerning payment for slaves enlisted into service would persist into the Jackson administration. Dutee Pearce would write to Daniel Updike in North Kingston of the long debate about "paying for an old negroe that Jackson empressed into his service, at New Orleans, and who died. The debate is becoming more and more animated," he wrote, and added deprecatingly that all the time consumed on the question "be worth more than I would give for all the negroes in the country." (RIHS) Shipley Collection, vol. 12: 115.

4. Rider, *An Historical Inquiry*, 84.

5. Quoted in Rider, *An Historical Inquiry*, 85.

6. John Wood Sweet, *Bodies Politic Negotiating Race in the American North, 1730–1830* (Baltimore: Johns Hopkins University Press, 2003), 254–255.

7. Bartlett, ed., *Records of the State of Rhode Island and Providence Plantations*, vol. 9, 485–487.

8. Irwin H. Polishook, *Rhode Island and the Union 1774–1795* (Evanston, Ill.: Northwestern University Press, 1969), 61.

9. Howard W. Preston, ed., *Autograph Letters and Documents of George Washington Now in Rhode Island Collections* (Providence: E. L. Freeman, 1932), 70–72.

10. James B. Hedges, *The Browns of Providence Plantations* (Cambridge, Mass.: Harvard University Press, 1952), 314.

11. Bartlett, *Records of the State of Rhode Island and Providence Plantations in New England*, vol. 10: 85.

12. Berlin, *The Long Emancipation*, 62–64.

13. Ibid., 75–76.

14. Peter J. Coleman, *The Transformation of Rhode Island 1790–1860* (Providence: Brown University Press, 1963), 51–57.

15. For an account of DeWolf's nearly lifelong activity in the slave trade, see Cynthia Mestad Johnson, *James DeWolf and the Rhode Island Slave Trade* (Charleston, S.C.: History Press, 2014).

16. I would recommend to the reader Joanne Pope Melish's *Disowning Slavery* as well as Ruth Wallis Herndon's *Unwelcome Americans* for a fuller understanding of the times and the measures meted out against the poor during this period.

17. See Neil Dunay, "Captives at Cocumscussoc: From Bondage to Freedom" from T. G. Cranston and Dunay, *We Were Here Too: Selected Stories of Black History in North Kingston* (Middletown, Del.: Create-Space, 2014), 84–88.

18. Ibid., 83.

19. Account books of Daniel Updike (5 volumes), 1791–1801, vol. 5, 22–27 RIHS MSS, 770.

20. Linda L. Mathew, "Gleanings from Rhode Island Town Records: Providence Town Council Records, 1770–1788," *Rhode Island Roots*, April 2006, 108.

21. Arnold, ed., *Vital Records of Rhode Island*, vol. 13, 362.

22. Mathew, "Gleanings from Rhode Island Town Records," 99.

23. See "A List of Slaves Inlisted" in the Appendix.

24. Mathew, "Gleanings from Rhode Island Town Records," 108–109.

25. Ibid.

26. Ibid.

27. Ibid., 110–111.

28. For an extensive account of the legend surrounding the raid and the men involved, see Christian McBurney, *Kidnapping the Enemy* (Yardley, Pa.: Westholme, 2014), 213–219.

29. Washington was loath to practice capital punishment against his troops except "for example," as noted. One of the handful of Rhode Islanders executed during the war was John Bushby, shot by a firing squad for desertion: "he had been three times under sentence of death for like offence and had been twice pardoned" (*Providence Gazette*, November 23, 1778); James N. Arnold, ed., *Vital Records of Rhode Island 1636–1880* (Providence: Narragansett Historical Register, 1903), vol. 13: 239.

30. For a more detailed history, see the work of Bruce MacGunnigle in *Rhode Island Roots*, and *Strolling in Historic East Greenwich*, 30–31.

31. Richard Greene was the son of John Greene of Potowomut. He married Sarah Fry, the daughter of that prominent family in 1745. Wilkins Updike in his *History of the Episcopal Church in Narragansett*,

Rhode Island (Boston: D. B. Updike, 1907), writes that Greene "owned a farm in Coventry which was large and valuable; another in West Greenwich. . . . That on which he resided was I have heard contained two thousand acres." Greene had sheep and horses and cattle "in great abundance," and while he was not part of the Narragansett Planter community, seems to have emulated the lifestyle accordingly. Updike notes that "His wines and furniture were imported from England. Servants, both white and colored were numerous. There was much splendor in his housekeeping for the times in which he lived," 378.

32. Taylor, *Runaways, Deserters, and Notorious Villains*, vol. 1: 41.

33. Robert Emlin, "A Grievance Immortalized," talk at the John Nicholas Brown Center, April 28, 2016.

34. Bartlett, *Records of the State of Rhode Island and Providence Plantations in New England*, vol. 10, p. 163.

35. See Melish, *Disowning Slavery*, 242.

36. D. H. Greene, *History of East Greenwich* (Providence: J. A. Reid, 1877), 54.

37. Updike, *The History of the Episcopal Church in Narragansett*, 177–178.

38. Piersen, *Black Yankees*, 118.

39. Henry Clay Oatley, Jr. and Cherry Fletcher Bamber, eds., *Daniel Stedman's Journal, 1826–1859* (Greenville: Rhode Island Genealogical Society, 2000), 150.

40. Fuller, *The History of Warwick, Rhode Island*, 188–189.

41. Bruce C. MacGunnigle, *Strolling in Historic East Greenwich* (East Greenwich, 2014), 37–38.

42. *Providence Gazette*, January 25, 1821.

43. Nell, *The Colored Patriots of the American Revolution*, 75.

44. Geake, *A History of the Narragansett Tribe*, 71.

45. *Narragansett Dawn*, vol. 1, no. 8, December 1935, 190.

46. Princess Redwing, Address before the Woonsocket Chapter of the DAR, November 18, 1940. Text is taken from the handwritten notes of Princess Redwing, now located in the archives of the Tomaquag Museum, Exeter, Rhode Island.

47. "DAR Women Hear Princess Describe Indian Folk Lore," *Woonsocket Call*, November 19, 1940, Archives of the Tomaquag Memorial Museum, Exeter, Rhode Island.

48. Cowell, *Spirit of '76*, 313.

49. James Wappy and his son James Jr. are both listed on the 1777 Military Census and James is listed in the DAR registry based upon records in the Rhode Island Revolutionary War Index. Neither man however, is listed in the Regimental book of the 1st Rhode Island Regiment.

50. See Mss 231 sg 3 series 1 General Assembly Box 3, Folder 15. Rhode Island State Records, Rhode Island Historical Society.

51. John Wood Sweet, *Bodies Politic: Negotiating Race in the American North, 1730–1830* (Baltimore: Johns Hopkins University Press, 2003), 324.

52. Alden G. Beaman, ed., *Rhode Island Vital Records* (East Princeton, Mass., 1981), 133.

53. See "Illegal Detribalization," Narragansett Indian Tribe website, www.narragansetttribe.org/illegal-detribalization.html.

54. Arnold, ed., *Vital Records of Rhode Island 1636–1880* (Providence: Narragansett Historical Register, 1903), vol. 12: 468.

55. Arnold, ed., *Vital Records of Rhode Island 1636–1880*, vol. 13: 342.

56. Arnold, ed., *Vital Records of Rhode Island 1636–1880*, vol. 19: 159.

FIVE: THE LEGACY OF THE 1ST RHODE ISLAND REGIMENT

1. Thayer had been the first "superintendent" of West Point, and under his tutelage the institution had become the nation's first college of engineering.

2. R. L. Murray, *A Perfect Storm of Lead: George Sears Greene's New York Brigade in Defense of Culp's Hill* (Wolcott, N.Y.: Benedum Books, 2000), 55.

3. As a historian, Bruce McGunnigle has written over 150 columns for the *East Greenwich Pendulum*, and the *Northeast Independent* since 2012. He first published work in 1977 is titled *Rhode Island Freemen 1747–1755: A Census of Registered Voters*, and later work would include a volume of transcriptions from the gravestones in historical cemeteries of East Greenwich, as well as the works cited in this book. As a genealogist, he contributes regularly to *Rhode Island Roots* magazine, the publication of the Rhode Island Genealogical Society. He is often a featured speaker at genealogical conventions, telling the story of Ichabod Northup, Winsor Fry, or Thomas Mitchell, those veterans of the 1st Rhode Island Regiment whose stories he came to know through his extensive research.

4. William Chenery, *The Fourteenth Regiment Rhode Island Heavy Artillery (Colored) in the War to Preserve the Union* (Providence: Snow & Farnum, 1898), 10.

5. Ibid., 66.

6. Letter from Nancy Brown-Garcia to the author, February 26, 2016.

7. Ibid.

8. Letter from Susan Holden to Governor John Brown Francis, concerning the origins of the Free Will Baptist Church and subscription to build a new church, transcribed by, and from the collection of Henry A. L. Brown. See also *Narragansett Historical Register* 7, no. 3 (Providence), July 1889.

9. At the time of this writing, the Yorktown Historical Museum is preparing to erect a monument to the soldiers at Pines Bridge in May of 2017. The monument will be the first to depict the multiracial roster of the 1st Rhode Island Regiment, and will bear an inscription written by Rhode Island historian Norm Demaris. The monument, as designed by Oregon-based sculptor Jay Warren, depicts three bronze statues of equal height representing the white, black, and indigenous soldiers as they stood together, back to back in a posture of last defense.

Selected Bibliography

Arnold, James N., ed. *Vital Records of Rhode Island 1636–1880*. Providence: Narragansett Historical Register, 1903.

Arnold, Samuel Greene. *The Centennial Celebration of the Battle of Rhode Island*. Historical Tract No. 8. Rhode Island Historical Society, 1878.

_____. *A History of the State of Rhode Island and Providence Plantations*. 2 vols. New York: D. Appleton & Co., 1874.

Bartlett, John Russell. *Records of the State of Rhode Island and Providence Plantations in New England*. 2 vols. Providence: General Assembly, 1865.

Berlin, Ira. *The Long Emancipation: The Demise of Slavery in the United States*. Cambridge, Mass.: Harvard University Press, 2015.

Cowell, Benjamin. *Spirit of '76 in Rhode Island: or Sketches of the Efforts of the Government and People in the War of Revolution*. Boston, 1850.

Cranston, G. Timothy, with Neil Dunay. *We Were Here Too, Selected Stories of Black History in North Kingstown*. North Kingstown: privately printed, 2015.

Denison, Frederic (Rev.). *Westerly Rhode Island and Its Witnesses, For Two Hundred and Fifty Years 1626–1876*. Providence: J. A. Reid, 1878.

Field, Edward, ed. *Diary of Colonel Israel Angell 1778–1781*. Providence: Preston and Rounds, 1899.

Fuller, Oliver Payson. *The History of Warwick, R.I.* Providence: Burlingame & Co., 1875.

Grundset, Eric G., ed. *Forgotten Patriots: African American and American Indian Patriots in the Revolutionary War.* Washington, D.C.: National Society of Daughters of the American Revolution, 2008.

Hoffer, Peter Charles. *Cry Liberty: The Great Stono River Slave Rebellion of 1730.* London: Oxford University Press, 2010.

Horne, Gerald. *The Counter-Revolution of 1776: Slave Resistance and the Origins of the United States of America.* New York: New York University Press, 2014.

Humphrey, William. *A Journal Made in the Year 1775–1776,* from *Rhode Islanders Record the Revolution: The Journals of William Humphrey and Zuriel Waterman.* Providence: Rhode Island Publications Society, 1984.

Ketchum, Richard M. *Victory at Yorktown: The Campaign that Won the Revolution.* New York: Henry Holt, 2004.

Mackenzie, Frederick. *Diary of Frederick MacKenzie Giving a Daily Narrative of his Military Service as an Officer of the Regiment of Royal Welch Fusiliers During The Years 1775–1781 in Massachusetts, Rhode Island and New York.* Cambridge, Mass.: Harvard University Press, 1930.

Martin, Joseph Plumb (George F. Sheer, ed.). *Private Yankee Doodle, Being a Narrative of Some of the Adventures, Dangers, and Sufferings of a Revolutionary Soldier.* Boston: Little, Brown, 1962.

Massey, Gregory D. and James Piecuch, eds. *General Nathanael Greene and the American Revolution in the South.* Columbia: University of South Carolina Press, 2012.

McBurney, Christian M. *The Rhode Island Campaign.* Yardley, Pa.: Westholme, 2011.

_____. *Rhode Island Spies in the Revolution.* Charleston, S.C.: History Press, 2014.

MacGunnigle, Bruce C. *Regimental Book Rhode Island Regiment for 1781 &c.* East Greenwich: Rhode Island Society of the Sons of the American Revolution, 2011.

———. *Strolling in Historic East Greenwich.* East Greenwich, 2014.

Piersen, William D. *Black Yankees.* Amherst: University of Massachusetts Press, 1988.

Polishook, Irwin H. *Rhode Island and the Union 1774–1795.* Evanston, Ill.: Northwestern University Press, 1969.

Quarles, Benjamin. *The Negro in the American Revolution.* Chapel Hill: University of North Carolina Press, 1961.

Taylor, Maureen. *Runaways, Deserters, and Notorious Villains.* 2 vols. Rockport: Picton Press, 1995.

Thatcher, James. *A Military Journal During the American Revolutionary War from 1775–1783.* 2nd ed. Plymouth: 1827.

Walker, Anthony. *So Few the Brave.* Newport: Seafield Press, 1981.

Woodward, Carl R. *Plantation in Yankeeland.* Wickford: Cocumscussoc Association, 1971.

Acknowledgments

THE AUTHOR WOULD FIRST AND FOREMOST LIKE TO thank my colleague Lorén M. Spears for her contributions of oral and written history to this book, as well as an indigenous perspective that was an essential element in telling the full story. I would also like to thank the Tomaquag Museum for their support, and for opening its archives for the research of this book, as well as their help in connecting the author with a number of tribal members whose ancestors had served in the Revolutionary War.

I would like to thank the staff of the Robinson Research Center of the Rhode Island Historical Society for assistance with locating documents, letters, and papers relevant to my research. I'd also like to thank the staff of the John Carter Brown Library at Brown University, especially Director Neil Safier for inviting Lorén Spears and myself to present our work in progress to Fellows and attendees, as well as Kimberly Nusco for locating materials related to the work.

My personal thanks go to those members of the Narragansett tribe who supported the work and provided needed material and counsel, including Paulla Dove Jennings, Dawn Dove, and Dr. Joyce Stevos. I would also like to thank Nancy Brown-Garcia of the National Algonqian Indian Council for her written and oral contributions as well as her counsel.

I especially wish to thank my friends at Smith's Castle and the Warwick Historical Society for their continued support, as well as Carl Becker, Henry A. L. Brown, Dr. Patrick Conley, G. Timothy Cranston, Neil Dunay, Linford Fisher, Christian McBurney, Bruce MacGunnigle, Rachel Pierce, Ray Rickman, Dr. William S. Simmons, Maureen Taylor, Ted Widmer, and Noreen O'Connor-Abel and Bruce H. Franklin of Westholme Publising, for their kind assistance, direction, or support as needed, that enabled the book to come to fruition.

Index